pasta & italian

ROBYN MARTIN

ISBN 1-877193-99-2

© Design and photography:
Concept Publishing
© Text: Robyn Martin

Published in 2000 by
Concept Publishing
Fax 64-9-489 5335
Auckland, New Zealand

READON
PUBLICATIONS
INCORPORATED

This edition published by
Readon Publications Inc
S/B 100 The East Mall, Unit # 15
Etobicoke, Ontario M8Z 5X2
Tel No. 416 503 3444
Toll Free No. 1-800-401-9774
Fax No. 416-503 9386
E-Mail Address: readon@platinuml.com
Website: www.readon.com

TEXT: Robyn Martin

IMPERIAL EDITION TEXT EDITED BY:
Barbara Gibbs Ostmann

PHOTOGRAPHY: Alan Gillard

COVER PHOTOGRAPH:
Pasta with Basil Pesto and parmesan cheese

DESIGN: Wandering Stars

PRODUCTION: Sue Attwood

RECIPES TESTED BY:
Virginia McGregor and Linda Laycock

PRINTED IN HONG KONG BY:
Bookbuilders

WEIGHTS AND MEASURES
All recipes in this book have been tested using standard
measuring cups and spoons. All cup and spoon measures
are level and brown sugar measures are firmly packed.

Medium-sized eggs are used.

contents

soups, snacks & pizzas

Everybody needs a repertoire of good ideas for easy snacks, nibbles and first courses. Time is always short when you're preparing for company, so these recipes are as quick as they are tasty.

pork and **rosemary** skewers

Ciabatta is an Italian bread. Focaccia will do just as well for this recipe.

24 satay sticks or wooden or bamboo skewers
1 pound piece boneless pork
6 slices bacon
4 sprigs fresh rosemary
3 tablespoons lemon juice
1 loaf ciabatta or focaccia bread
$\frac{1}{2}$ cup red currant or rosemary jelly, or other tart jelly
4 red bell peppers, roasted
Small salad greens

Soak satay sticks or skewers in water for 30 minutes before using. Cut pork lengthwise into four pieces. Cut into 1-inch cubes. Cut each slice of bacon crosswise into four pieces. Tightly roll up each piece. Cut rosemary sprigs into 1-inch pieces. Thread a pork cube and a bacon roll onto each stick, and wedge a piece of rosemary in between. Repeat once more for each skewer. Brush with lemon juice. Broil skewers for 10 minutes, turning regularly, until meat is just cooked. Cut ciabatta in half horizontally. Toast both sides of bread under broiler. When ready to serve, spread rosemary jelly on bread and top with strips of roasted red bell peppers, salad greens and cooked pork skewers.

Makes 24.

pork and rosemary skewers

antipasto platter

Open your pantry and be creative with whatever you have on hand to create an imaginative, well-presented and appetizing antipasto platter.

SOME PANTRY BASICS
Sun-dried tomatoes
Olives
Sliced salami
Sliced pastrami
Dolmades
Artichokes
Pickled bell peppers
Roasted bell peppers
Marinated mussels
Capers
Sliced brie or camembert cheese

THE THINGS TO MAKE

Wedges of Frittata (page 11)
Crostini (page 7)
Marinated Mushrooms (page 7)
Marinated Olives (page 6)

Arrange a selection of ready-to-eat morsels on a platter. Accompany with spoons or forks for serving. Small plates and napkins are useful for guests to use.

marinated olives

Make your own special brew of olives for simple alfresco eating. This is not a recipe for preparing fresh olives.

2 cups ripe (black) olives
5 cloves garlic
2 tablespoons fresh rosemary leaves
About 1½ cups olive oil

Wash and dry olives. Crush and peel garlic. Blanch garlic and rosemary in boiling water for 1 minute. Pack olives into clean, dry jars. Divide garlic and rosemary among jars. Add enough olive oil to completely cover olives and herbs. Seal jars. Refrigerate and use within one week.

Makes 2½ cups.

antipasto platter with marinated olives, bruschetta, crostini, roasted bell peppers and marinated mushrooms

bruschetta

Thick slices of bread
1 clove garlic
Olive oil

Broil bread slices on both sides until crisp and dry. Crush and peel garlic. Rub garlic over bread. Drizzle olive oil over bread. Spread with pesto, pickle, dressing or any other suitable spread. Top with anything from sliced hard-cooked egg to sliced cold meats, tomato slices, roasted bell peppers or other toppings. Serve as a dunker for dips.

crostini

Small rounds or squares of bread
Olive oil or melted butter

Brush bread with olive oil or melted butter. Broil until lightly toasted or bake at 375°F for 5 minutes. Top with toppings of your choice as for Bruschetta or serve with dips or as part of an antipasto platter.

roasted bell peppers

3 red bell peppers
3 green bell peppers

Bake bell peppers at 400°F for 10 minutes, or until skin blisters and starts to blacken. Remove from oven and wrap in paper or a paper bag until cool enough to handle. Remove skins. Cut peppers into thin strips, removing core.

marinated mushrooms

These can be served as a salad if wished but they make a delicious addition to an antipasto platter.

4 ounces fresh button mushrooms
1 small clove garlic
¼ cup olive oil
2 tablespoons lemon juice
¼ teaspoon dried marjoram
Freshly ground black pepper

If mushrooms are very small, leave whole. It not, slice thin. Crush and peel garlic and cut into slivers. Mix mushrooms, garlic, olive oil, lemon juice, marjoram and pepper together. Let marinate in refrigerator for at least 2 hours or overnight. Serve as part of an antipasto platter.

Serves 6.

7

breads with flavored oils

Flavored oils are available in some supermarkets or in good delicatessens. They are very easy to make at home to have as part of your basic "finger food" pantry.

lemon and garlic oil

1 cup olive oil
1 lemon
1 large clove garlic

Place a clean bottle in the oven at 250°F for 20 minutes. Thinly cut peel from lemon, making sure there is no white pith on it. Cut peel into thin strips. Crush and peel garlic. Put lemon peel and garlic into the warm bottle. Pour in olive oil. Seal with a stopper. Refrigerate and use within one week.

Makes 1 cup.

basil oil

2 cups fresh basil leaves
1 teaspoon salt
2 cups olive oil

Wash and dry basil. Place basil, salt and oil in a food processor or blender. Process or blend until coarsely chopped. Pour into hot, clean, dry jars or bottles. Seal. Refrigerate and use within one week.

Makes 2$\frac{1}{2}$ cups.

TO SERVE FLAVORED OILS

Pour oil into a small bowl. Serve with bite-sized pieces of bread.

lemon and garlic oil, basil pesto, basil oil and quick pizza dough

quick **pizza** dough

This pizza dough has all the flavor of a traditional yeast dough but requires no rising.

1 teaspoon granulated sugar
1/2 cup warm water
1 1/2 teaspoons active dry yeast
1 cup self-rising flour
1/4 cup bread flour
1/4 teaspoon salt
1 tablespoon olive oil

Dissolve sugar in water. Sprinkle yeast over water and let stand for 10 minutes or until frothy. Mix self-rising flour, bread flour and salt together in a bowl. Make a well in the center and add olive oil and yeast mixture. Mix well, adding extra flour if necessary. Knead on a floured surface until smooth and elastic, adding more flour if necessary. Use to make pizza, with topping of your choice, or pizza bread or calzone.

Makes enough dough for a 12-inch diameter pizza.

basil **pesto**

3/4 cup tightly packed fresh basil leaves
1 clove garlic
Pinch salt
1/4 cup olive oil, divided
1/4 cup toasted pine nuts
2 tablespoons grated parmesan cheese

Place basil in the bowl of a food processor or in a mortar. Crush and peel garlic. Add garlic to basil along with salt and half of the oil. Process, or pound with a pestle, to a smooth paste. Add pine nuts and remaining oil; process or pound until nuts are lightly chopped. Add parmesan cheese and process to mix in. Use as wished. To store pesto, pour into a container, smooth surface and pour extra olive oil over the top. Cover and refrigerate for up to a week, or freeze in small blocks or in ice-cube trays.

Makes about 3/4 cup.

9

quick pizza toppings

rajah's **pizza**

Spread pizza base made from Quick Pizza Dough (page 9) with cream cheese. Cover with chutney. Brush chicken tenderloins with a wet tandoori spice mix. Pile chicken onto pizza. Bake at 400°F for 15 to 20 minutes, or until chicken is cooked. Serve with yogurt and chopped fresh coriander (cilantro).

blt and **pineapple** pizza

Roll up bacon slices. Secure with a wooden toothpick if necessary. Spread pizza base made from Quick Pizza Dough (page 9) with tomato paste. Sprinkle with grated cheese. Top with bacon rolls, pineapple pieces and chopped tomato. Bake at 400°F for 15 to 20 minutes, or until golden and bacon is cooked. Top with shredded lettuce and mayonnaise.

simple artichoke **pizza**

Spread pizza base made from Quick Pizza Dough (page 9) with tomato paste, sprinkle with grated cheese, top with drained, halved, canned artichoke hearts and sprinkle with chopped parsley and oregano. Bake at 400°F for 10 to 15 minutes.

pizza bread

1 recipe Quick Pizza Dough (page 9)
2 tablespoons olive oil
2 cloves garlic
Coarse salt

Prepare pizza dough according to recipe. Divide dough in half. Roll each half into a 6-inch-diameter circle. Place dough circles on an oiled baking sheet. Brush olive oil on dough. Crush and peel garlic and chop fine. Sprinkle garlic and a little coarse salt over dough. Bake at 400°F for 10 to 15 minutes, or until golden and crisp. Cut into wedges.

Serves 6.

from top left clockwise, rajah's pizza, pizza bread, blt and pineapple pizza and simple artichoke pizza

cheese and
bacon **pierogi**

2 recipes Quick Pizza Dough (page 9)
6 slices bacon
4 ounces double-cream camembert
  cheese
1 egg
1 tablespoon water

Prepare two batches of pizza dough
according to recipe directions. Cut bacon
into $^1/_2$-inch-wide strips. Cut camembert
cheese into $^1/_2$-inch cubes. Form dough
into a 9-inch-long cylinder. Cut 1-inch
pieces from cylinder. Form one piece into
a ball and flatten it in the palm of your
hand. Place a piece of bacon and a cube
of camembert cheese in the center of the
dough round. Wrap dough around bacon
and cheese to form a ball. Repeat with
remaining dough, bacon and cheese.
Lightly beat egg and water together.
Brush pierogi with egg wash or dip them
into it. Place on a greased baking sheet.
Bake at 450°F for 10 to 15 minutes, or
until golden and cooked. Serve warm.

Makes 28.

bell pepper and potato frittata,
cheese and bacon pierogi and
mozzarella and sage puffs

mozzarella and **sage** puffs

2 green onions
1 cup grated mozzarella cheese
2 eggs
¼ cup all-purpose flour
1 teaspoon dried sage
About 1 cup vegetable oil

Trim green onions and slice fine. Mix green onions, cheese, eggs, flour and sage together until combined. Heat oil in a skillet. Drop rounded teaspoons of batter into oil. Cook, turning often, until golden. Drain on paper towels. Serve hot. To reheat, place in a 400°F oven for 3 to 4 minutes.

Makes about 20.

bell pepper and potato **frittata**

Use leftover cooked vegetables for this if preferred or if that is what you have on hand.

2 potatoes
1 zucchini
2 red bell peppers, roasted
4 eggs
Salt
Freshly ground black pepper
3 tablespoons vegetable oil

Peel and grate potatoes. Trim and grate zucchini. Cut bell peppers into thin strips. Lightly beat eggs. Season with salt and pepper. Stir in potatoes, zucchini and peppers. Heat oil in a large skillet. Pour in egg mixture. Cook over medium heat for about 8 minutes, or until egg is set. Cut in half and turn to cook other side until golden. To serve, cut into small wedges. Serve warm or cold.

Makes 16 wedges.

roasted mushroom tapenade

roasted mushroom
tapenade

**8 ounces fresh brown button
  mushrooms**
4 cloves garlic
2 tablespoons olive oil
$\frac{1}{2}$ cup pitted ripe (black) olives
2 slices stale white bread
4 slices chili pepper salami
1 tablespoon chopped fresh parsley

Wipe mushrooms and trim stems if
necessary. Place mushrooms, garlic and oil
in a shallow baking dish. Bake at 350°F
for 15 minutes. Place mushrooms and
olives in a food processor or blender.
Squeeze garlic pulp from skin and add
pulp to mushrooms. Remove crusts from
bread. Coarsely chop salami. Add bread
and salami to mushrooms. Process until
smooth. Place in a serving bowl and
garnish with chopped parsley.

Makes 1 cup.

ratatouille rolls

1 small eggplant
$\frac{1}{2}$ cup sun-dried tomato pesto
12 slices pepper jack cheese
6 ounces smoked ham, sliced
Olive oil
Wooden toothpicks

Using a wide peeler, cut eggplant into
thin lengthwise slices. Thinly spread slices
with pesto. Cut cheese and ham to fit
eggplant slices. Place over pesto. Roll up
eggplant, starting from the short side.
Secure with a toothpick. Brush rolls with
oil. Bake at 375°F for 5 minutes, or until
eggplant is tender. Cut in half to serve.

Makes about 24.

capable
devils on horseback

24 pitted prunes
$\frac{1}{4}$ cup capers
12 slices bacon
24 wooden toothpicks

Open prunes at pit cavity. Fill with three
or four capers. Fold prune to enclose
capers. Cut bacon in half lengthwise. Roll
a bacon slice around each prune. Secure
with a toothpick. Broil until bacon is
cooked, turning during cooking. Serve
warm.

Makes 24.

capable devils on horseback
and ratatouille rolls

sage and pea **chicken** roll-ups

If schnitzels are not available, buy boned, skinned chicken breasts. Slit them horizontally and spread them open, then beat with a meat mallet, bottle or rolling pin to flatten.

1 cup cooked peas
1 small onion
1 teaspoon dried sage
1 teaspoon chicken bouillon granules
1 cup soft bread crumbs
1 egg
9 chicken schnitzels
2 tablespoons vegetable oil

Mash peas or process in a food processor. Peel onion and chop fine. Mix peas, onion, sage, bouillon granules, bread crumbs and egg together. Divide mixture among schnitzels, placing lengthwise down the center of each schnitzel. Roll meat around stuffing. Secure with toothpicks if necessary. Heat oil in a skillet. Brown chicken rolls in oil. Cover with a lid or foil and cook over low heat for 4 minutes, or until cooked. Cut into slices to serve hot or cold.

Makes 27.

**sage and pea chicken roll-ups,
frank's rolls and pepperoni toasties**

frank's **rolls**

What could be faster than this in the homemade and delicious-tasting sausage roll stakes?

1 sheet pre-rolled flaky puff pastry
2 tablespoons fruit chutney
6 frankfurters
1 egg yolk
1 tablespoon water
$1/2$ teaspoon prepared mustard

Place pastry sheet on a cutting board and cut it into thirds. Spread fruit chutney to within $1/2$ inch of long edges of each piece of pastry. Place two frankfurters down center of each piece of pastry. Wet pastry edges, roll pastry over filling and press overlapping edges of pastry together. Mix egg yolk, water and mustard together. Brush rolls with egg wash. Cut rolls into $1 1/4$-inch lengths. Place on an ungreased baking sheet and bake at 400°F for 15 minutes, or until golden and cooked.

Makes 18.

pepperoni **toasties**

10 slices whole wheat sandwich bread
$1/2$ of an 8-ounce package cream cheese, softened
4 ounces pepperoni, sliced
2 hard-cooked eggs
6 gherkins
$1/2$ cup mayonnaise
$1/2$ cup low-fat sour cream
Oil spray

Cut crusts from bread. Spread cream cheese on one side of each slice of bread. Place two pepperoni slices diagonally on each slice of bread. Peel eggs and coarsely chop. Chop gherkins. Mix mayonnaise, sour cream, eggs and gherkins together. Divide mixture among bread slices and spread over pepperoni slices. Roll up each slice of bread on the diagonal and secure with toothpicks. Spray with oil and place on a baking sheet. Bake at 350°F for 12 minutes, or until bread is golden and crisp. Cut rolls in half and serve warm.

Makes 20.

mediterranean tomato and **cheese tarts**

3 sheets phyllo pastry
1/2 cup soft bread crumbs
2 cups grated gouda cheese
2 small tomatoes
Salt
Black pepper
Fresh basil leaves

Place one sheet of pastry on a large board. Sprinkle half the bread crumbs on pastry. Top with a second sheet of pastry. Sprinkle remaining bread crumbs on pastry. Top with third sheet of pastry. Cut layered pastry into 10 (3 1/2-inch) squares. Place each layered square in a greased muffin or tart pan, turning each layer so the corners don't line up. Divide cheese among pastry cases. Remove stem end from tomatoes and cut into slices. Cut slices in half. Arrange two pieces of tomato on top of cheese in each tart. Sprinkle with salt and pepper. Bake at 400°F for 12 to 15 minutes, or until pastry is cooked and golden. Cool slightly. Place on a serving plate. Tear basil leaves and scatter over tarts. Serve warm.

Makes 12.

crostini with **chickpeas** and tomato

1/2 loaf French bread
1 (15-ounce) can chickpeas or
**   garbanzo beans**
1 tablespoon basil pesto
1/2 teaspoon salt
4 medium tomatoes
Freshly ground black pepper
Fresh marjoram leaves

Cut bread into 1/2-inch slices. Place on an ungreased baking sheet and bake at 350°F for 5 to 10 minutes, or until lightly golden. Let cool and store in an airtight container until ready to use. Drain chickpeas. Place chickpeas, pesto and salt in a food processor or blender and process until coarsely chopped and mixed. Slice tomatoes. Pile about a tablespoon of chickpea mixture on each crostini. Top each with a slice of tomato. Grind pepper over all and garnish with marjoram.

Makes about 24.

**crostini with chickpeas and tomato, and
mediterranean tomato and cheese tarts**

finger **spinach** pies

1 (10-ounce) package frozen spinach
1 small onion
1 tablespoon vegetable oil
1 egg
Pinch ground nutmeg
$\frac{1}{2}$ teaspoon salt
Freshly ground black pepper
$\frac{1}{4}$ cup plain yogurt
3 sheets phyllo pastry
$\frac{1}{4}$ cup olive oil, divided

Thaw spinach and drain well. Peel onion
and chop fine. Heat vegetable oil; add
onion and cook and stir for 3 to 4 minutes.
Add onion mixture to spinach along with
egg, nutmeg, salt, pepper and yogurt.
Mix to combine. Place one sheet of
phyllo pastry on a cutting board. Brush
pastry with olive oil and fold in half
lengthwise. Spread a $\frac{1}{2}$-inch-wide strip
of spinach mixture down one long edge
of the pastry, to within $\frac{1}{2}$ inch of ends.
Fold up ends, then roll up pastry from
the long side. Coil the spinach roll, like a
snail. Repeat with remaining phyllo and
spinach mixture. Place coils in an oiled
baking dish. Brush with olive oil. Bake at
375°F for 25 minutes, or until golden and
cooked. Cut into quarters to serve.

Makes 3 coils.

finger spinach pies, roasted bell
pepper and sun-dried tomato pate,
roasted eggplant dip or spread

roasted bell pepper and sun-dried **tomato pate**

2 red bell peppers
$\frac{1}{2}$ cup drained sun-dried tomatoes
   in oil
1 teaspoon unflavored gelatin
1 tablespoon water
$\frac{1}{2}$ cup plain yogurt

Cut bell peppers in half and remove
seeds. Place peppers cut-side down on an
ungreased baking sheet. Broil until skins
are golden and blistered. Let cool, then
remove skins. Place peppers and
tomatoes in a blender or food processor
and blend until smooth. Soak gelatin in
water for 2 to 3 minutes; dissolve over
hot water. Add gelatin to bell pepper
mixture along with yogurt; mix until
combined. Place in a serving bowl, mold
or small loaf pan. Serve with vegetables
or bread.

Makes 1$\frac{1}{4}$ cups.

roasted **eggplant** dip or spread

1 medium eggplant
2 tablespoons olive oil, divided
1 small onion
1 clove garlic
$\frac{1}{2}$ cup soft white bread crumbs
$\frac{1}{4}$ cup plain yogurt
$\frac{1}{4}$ cup finely chopped fresh parsley

Cut eggplant into $^3/_4$-inch-thick slices.
Place on an ungreased baking sheet.
Brush with oil and broil until lightly
golden. Turn and brush uncooked side
with oil. Broil until golden. Let cool, then
remove skin. Place eggplant in a blender
or food processor. Peel onion and
coarsely chop. Crush and peel garlic. Add
onion and garlic to eggplant along with
bread crumbs, yogurt and parsley. Blend
until combined. Serve with pita crisps.

Makes 1$\frac{1}{4}$ cups.

creamy **eggplant** topping

1 medium eggplant
3 cloves garlic
2 tablespoons olive oil
2 tablespoons lemon juice
Salt
Freshly ground black pepper
Bruschetta or crostini
Fresh basil leaves

Place eggplant and unpeeled garlic on an ungreased baking sheet and broil under a hot broiler, turning until eggplant is black on all sides. Take care not to puncture eggplant. Turn garlic regularly and remove from broiler if skin starts to brown. When eggplant is black and soft, remove from oven. Let cool. Remove eggplant skin. Drain eggplant if necessary, then mash. Peel garlic and mash with eggplant. Add olive oil, lemon juice, salt and pepper to eggplant puree. Mix well. Use to top bruschetta or crostini. Garnish with torn basil leaves.

Makes about 1½ cups.

chili **broccoli** spread

3 cloves garlic
1 pound fresh broccoli
1 tablespoon olive oil
¼ teaspoon chili powder
¾ cup boiling water
Salt
Bruschetta or crostini
3 to 4 ripe (black) olives

Crush and peel garlic and chop fine. Trim broccoli and cut into florets. Heat oil in a saucepan. Add garlic and cook over low heat for 2 minutes. Add chili powder and cook and stir for 1 minute, or until garlic and chili are fragrant. Add broccoli, water and salt. Cover and cook over medium heat for about 10 minutes, or until broccoli is just cooked. Remove lid. Mash broccoli with a potato masher. Continue cooking over low heat, mashing regularly, until water has evaporated and broccoli has formed a coarse puree. Use to top bruschetta or crostini and garnish with sliced olives.

Makes 1½ cups.

roasted
bell pepper topping

2 red bell peppers
1 yellow bell pepper
1 green bell pepper
1 clove garlic
1 tablespoon olive oil
1 tablespoon white vinegar
Freshly ground black pepper
Bruschetta or crostini

Cut bell peppers in half lengthwise. Remove seeds and stems. Place peppers cut-side down on an ungreased baking sheet and broil until skin is blistered and brown. Wrap in foil and let cool. Remove skins. Cut peppers into thin strips. Crush and peel garlic and chop fine. Mix bell pepper strips, garlic, oil, vinegar and pepper together. Use to top bruschetta or crostini.

Makes about 1$\frac{1}{2}$ cups.

bruschetta and crostini (recipe page 7) with chili broccoli spread, creamy eggplant topping and roasted bell pepper topping

tuscan **pizzettes**

**1 recipe Quick Pizza Dough
   (page 9)**
3 tablespoons basil pesto
4 slices bacon
2 tomatoes

Prepare pizza dough according to recipe. Form dough into a 1^1/$_4$-inch-diameter cylinder. Cut or break cylinder into ^{1}/$_2$-inch-wide slices. Form each piece of dough into a round and place on an ungreased baking sheet. Spread pesto on dough rounds. Cut bacon into ^{1}/$_2$-inch-wide strips. Criss-cross two strips on each round. Slice tomatoes. Place a tomato slice on each round. Bake at 400°F for 10 minutes, or until pizzettes are cooked.

Makes about 28.

bengal **pizzettes**

1 recipe Quick Pizza Dough (page 9)
3 tablespoons mango chutney
1 smoked chicken breast
^{1}/$_2$ cup plain yogurt
**^{1}/$_4$ cup chopped green onions
   (green part only)**

Prepare pizza dough according to recipe. Form dough into a 1^1/$_4$-inch-diameter cylinder. Cut or break cylinder into ^{1}/$_2$-inch-wide slices. Form each piece of dough into a round and place on an ungreased baking sheet. Spread chutney on dough rounds. Remove skin and bone from chicken breast. Cut meat into chunks. Place chicken on top of chutney. Bake at 400°F for 10 minutes or until pizzettes are cooked. Remove from oven and spoon a teaspoon of yogurt over each pizzette. Top with green onions and serve.

Makes about 28.

quick pizza **pastry bites**

4 small tomatoes
**4 sheets unsweetened short pastry
   (your favorite recipe, or use
   refrigerated pizza crusts)**
^{1}/$_4$ cup tomato paste
^{1}/$_2$ teaspoon dried basil
^{1}/$_2$ teaspoon dried oregano
1 cup grated sharp cheddar cheese
2 slices bacon

Thinly slice tomatoes, then cut slices in half. Place two sheets of pastry on a cutting board. Spread each sheet with tomato paste and sprinkle with basil and oregano. Place remaining sheets on top to make two pastry "sandwiches." Sprinkle pastry tops with cheese, pressing cheese lightly into surface. Divide tomato slices evenly over cheese. Coarsely chop bacon. Sprinkle bacon over tomato. Cut each pastry sandwich into quarters, then cut each quarter in half on the diagonal, then cut each triangle in half, to make 32 triangles. Place on an ungreased baking sheet and bake at 425°F for 10 to 15 minutes, or until pastry is golden and bacon is cooked.

Makes 32.

toasted **pita bites**

6 small pita (pocket) breads
2 wedges blue cheese
1 cup walnut pieces, toasted
1 tablespoon vegetable oil

Cut a slit in the side of each pita bread. Mash cheese. Finely chop walnut pieces. Reserve ^{1}/$_4$ cup of walnuts for topping; mix remaining walnuts into cheese. Fill pita breads with cheese mixture. Brush top of pita breads with oil and sprinkle reserved walnuts over them. Place pita breads on an ungreased baking sheet and bake at 350°F for 8 to 10 minutes. Cut each pita bread into six wedges. Serve warm.

Makes 36.

toasted pita bites, tuscan pizzettes,
bengal pizzettes and quick pizza pastry bites

italian **ribollita**

2 onions
2 carrots
2 ribs celery
2 cloves garlic
2 zucchini
8 ounces fresh spinach
6 large tomatoes
2 tablespoons olive oil
3 tablespoons chopped fresh parsley
6 cups water
2 tablespoons tomato paste
Salt
Black pepper
3 slices stale bread, cut into cubes
Shaved parmesan cheese

Peel onions and carrots and chop very
fine. Trim celery. Crush and peel garlic.
Finely chop celery and garlic. Trim
zucchini and cut into cubes. Wash spinach
and remove stems. Cut tomatoes into
cubes, removing stem end. Heat oil in a
large saucepan and add onions, carrots,
celery, garlic and parsley. Cook and stir
over medium heat for about 7 minutes,
or until soft. Add zucchini, spinach and
tomatoes to saucepan along with water
and tomato paste. Cover and cook for
about 20 minutes, or until vegetables are
mushy. Season with salt and pepper. Add
bread and cook for 20 minutes. Thin with
hot water if necessary. Serve garnished
with parmesan cheese if wished.

Serves 6.

left: italian ribollita
right: minestrone with pesto cheese rolls

minestrone with pesto cheese rolls

Many versions of Minestrone abound from different parts of Italy. Here's mine.

2 carrots

3 ribs celery

2 onions

2 cloves garlic

2 tablespoons vegetable oil

1 (14- to 16-ounce) can tomatoes in juice

3 tablespoons tomato paste

6 cups vegetable stock

1 bouquet garni

1 (15- to 16-ounce) can red kidney beans

$^1/_2$ teaspoon salt

Black pepper

$^1/_4$ of a small green cabbage

8 ounces tagliatelle

Parmesan cheese

Wash and dice carrots and celery. Peel and slice onions. Crush, peel and chop garlic. Heat oil in a large saucepan. Add carrots, celery, onions and garlic and cook for about 5 minutes. Chop and core tomatoes. Add tomatoes with their juice, tomato paste, vegetable stock and bouquet garni to saucepan. Bring to the boil and simmer for 20 minutes, or until carrots are tender. Drain kidney beans and add to soup. Season to taste with salt and pepper. Core and thinly slice cabbage. Cut tagliatelle into 2$^1/_2$-inch lengths. Add cabbage and pasta to soup and cook for 5 minutes, or until tagliatelle is cooked. Remove bouquet garni. Garnish with grated or shaved parmesan cheese and serve with Pesto Cheese Rolls.

pesto cheese rolls

7 ounces savory short pastry (your favorite recipe, or use refrigerated pie crusts)

$^1/_4$ cup basil pesto

$^1/_4$ cup grated parmesan cheese

Roll out pastry to an 12 x 8-inch rectangle on a lightly floured surface. Spread with pesto and sprinkle with parmesan cheese. Trim edges to straighten. Cut pastry into 1-inch-wide strips and roll from the long side to enclose filling. Place on an ungreased baking sheet and bake at 375°F for 20 minutes, or until lightly golden.

Makes 12 rolls.

white bean
and sausage soup

2 onions
2 carrots
2 ribs celery
3 cloves garlic
1 tablespoon butter
1 bouquet garni
4 cups chicken stock
1(15- to 16-ounce) can cannellini-style
  butter beans
4 fancy sausages, such as chorizo,
  cooked
Salt
Black pepper
Roasted red bell pepper slices

Peel onions and coarsely chop. Peel carrots and chop. Trim celery and slice. Crush, peel and chop garlic. Heat butter in a large saucepan. Add onions, carrots, celery and garlic and cook for 10 minutes, taking care to not let vegetables color. Add bouquet garni and chicken stock. Bring to the boil and simmer for 10 minutes. Drain beans and add to saucepan. Puree mixture in a blender until smooth. Cut cooked sausages into $1/2$-inch slices. Reheat soup and add sausage slices, reserving a few for garnish. Season soup to taste. Serve piping hot garnished with red bell pepper and reserved sausage slices.

Serves 4.

absolutely scrumptious
watercress soup

The first time I made this soup was nearly the last. I carelessly didn't put the lid on my blender properly and ended up with a watercress redecoration of my kitchen – not a good look – plus a badly burnt hand and arm, so take care.

1 onion
1 leek
1 clove garlic
4 medium potatoes
Small bunch watercress
2 tablespoons butter
4 cups chicken stock
1 cup dry white wine
Salt
Black pepper
$1/2$ cup low-fat sour cream
Fresh herbs

Peel onion and chop. Trim leek and coarsely chop. Crush and peel garlic. Peel potatoes and cut into small pieces. Wash and drain watercress. Melt butter in a large saucepan. Add onion, leek, garlic and potatoes and cook for 5 minutes, or until onion is transparent. Add chicken stock and wine. Bring to the boil and simmer for 15 minutes. Add watercress and cook, skimming if necessary. Place soup in a blender, in batches if necessary, and blend until smooth. Return to saucepan. Reheat and season to taste with salt and pepper. Garnish with sour cream and fresh herbs.

Serves 4.

**white bean and sausage soup and
absolutely scrumptious watercress soup**

quick tomato and **basil** soup

1 onion
1 clove garlic
2 tablespoons vegetable oil
**1 (14- to 16-ounce) can tomatoes
   in juice**
1 (15-ounce) can tomato sauce
1 teaspoon dried basil
2 cups chicken stock
Freshly ground black pepper

Peel onion and chop fine. Crush, peel
and chop garlic. Heat oil in a large
saucepan. Add onion and garlic and cook
until transparent. Cut tomatoes into
quarters, removing cores. Add tomatoes
with their juice, tomato sauce, basil and
chicken stock to saucepan. Bring to the
boil and simmer for 5 minutes. Season
with freshly ground black pepper. Serve
immediately.

Serves 4.

lentil soup

1 cup brown lentils
1 large onion
2 cloves garlic
3 slices bacon
2 tablespoons vegetable oil
**1 (14- to 16-ounce) can
seasoned tomatoes**
**1 (14- to 16-ounce) can
tomatoes in juice**
1 teaspoon dried basil
6 cups beef stock

Soak lentils in water to cover
while preparing the rest of
the ingredients. Peel onion
and slice fine. Crush and peel
garlic and chop fine. Cut bacon
into small pieces. Heat oil in a
large saucepan. Add onion and
garlic and cook until transparent.
Add bacon and lightly cook. Drain
lentils. Add lentils, seasoned tomatoes
with their juice, tomatoes with their
juice, basil and beef stock. Cover and
cook for 1 to 1$\frac{1}{2}$ hours, or until lentils
are tender. Serve hot with crusty bread.

Serves 6.

lentil soup and quick tomato basil soup

tuscan **bean** soup

1 cup haricot beans
2 cloves garlic
¼ teaspoon salt
1 onion
3 ribs celery
1 leek
2 carrots
8 ounces fresh spinach
2 tablespoons vegetable oil
1 (6-ounce) can tomato paste
1 (14- to 16-ounce) can tomatoes
   in juice
1 cup beef stock
1 cup water
1 teaspoon dried thyme
Salt
Freshly ground black pepper

Soak beans overnight in water to cover. Drain beans. Add fresh water to cover; bring to the boil, then reduce heat and simmer for about 1 hour, or until just tender. While beans are cooking, crush and peel garlic, then mash it with salt. Peel and finely chop onion. Slice celery and leek. Peel and chop carrots. Wash spinach; remove stems and slice leaves. Heat oil in a large saucepan. Add garlic mixture, onion, celery, leek and carrots. Cover and cook, shaking pan frequently, until vegetables are golden. Stir in tomato paste, tomatoes with their juice, beef stock, 1 cup water and thyme. Bring to the boil. Cover and cook gently for 45 minutes. Drain beans, reserving ½ cup of cooking liquid. Put three-fourths of the beans into a blender or food processor along with the reserved ½ cup liquid. Process until very finely chopped. Add chopped beans and spinach to soup. Cook for 15 minutes. Add remaining whole cooked beans. Cook for 5 minutes. Season with salt and pepper. Serve with crusty bread.

Serves 6.

tuscan bean soup

pumpkin and
split pea soup

Use cold chicken stock for this recipe as hot stock will make the split peas hard.

1 onion
2 cloves garlic
1 (16- to 18-ounce) pumpkin
2 tablespoons vegetable oil
1 cup yellow split peas
5 cups cold chicken stock
Salt
Black pepper
Pinch ground nutmeg
Pesto, for garnish

Peel and chop onion. Crush, peel and chop garlic. Peel and seed pumpkin and cut into small pieces. Heat oil in a large saucepan. Add onion and garlic and cook and stir until clear. Add split peas and chicken stock. Bring to the boil, then add pumpkin. Cover and simmer for 30 to 40 minutes, or until peas are tender and pumpkin is breaking up. Stir to break up pumpkin. Season to taste with salt, pepper and nutmeg. Serve garnished with a swirl of pesto.

Serves 4.

pumpkin and split pea soup

the main course

While it's the feature act of any meal, a stunning main course doesn't have to be hard work. Simplicity is the starting point of style – that means building on natural flavors and finding delicious partnerships.

roasted bell pepper
casserole

When bell peppers are cheap, roast them and freeze them for use in the winter when they're pricey. Use a potato peeler to make parmesan cheese shavings.

3 red bell peppers
2 onions
3 cloves garlic
1 tablespoon vegetable oil
Pinch ground red (cayenne) pepper
2 tablespoons tomato paste
3/4 cup dry white wine or chicken stock
4 boneless chicken breast fillets
Salt
Freshly ground black pepper
Shaved parmesan cheese
Chopped fresh chives

Cut bell peppers in half vertically and remove seeds. Broil peppers on a baking sheet until skins blister. Remove from oven, let cool and peel off skin. Peel and chop onions. Crush and peel garlic. Heat oil in a skillet. Add onion and garlic and cook until onion is clear. Place roasted bell peppers, onion, garlic, ground red pepper and tomato paste in a blender or food processor and puree. Add wine and pulse to blend. Remove skin from chicken. Place chicken in a shallow baking dish. Pour bell pepper mixture over chicken. Cover and bake at 350°F for 20 to 25 minutes, or until chicken is cooked. Season with salt and pepper. Garnish with parmesan cheese and chives.

Serves 4.

roasted bell pepper casserole

liguria roast **chicken**

The origins of pesto are attributed to Liguria, a region in Northern Italy where the warm summer climate is obviously perfect for growing basil.

1 whole chicken
1/4 cup pesto
Shaved parmesan cheese

Truss chicken by tucking chicken wings under the back and tying chicken legs together. Generously brush pesto all over chicken. Bake at 350ºF for 1 hour, or until juices run clear when tested. Serve immediately, garnished with parmesan cheese.

PESTO
3/4 cup tightly packed fresh basil
 leaves
1 clove garlic
Pinch salt
1/4 cup olive oil, divided
1/4 cup pine nuts, toasted
2 tablespoons grated
 parmesan cheese

Place basil in the bowl of a food processor or in a mortar. Crush and peel garlic. Add garlic to basil along with salt and half of the oil. Process, or pound with a pestle, to a smooth paste. Add pine nuts and remaining oil and process or pound until nuts are lightly chopped. Add parmesan cheese and process until mixed. This recipe makes about 3/4 cup. Store extra pesto in refrigerator for up to a week, covering it with extra olive oil. Or, freeze in small blocks or in ice-cube trays.

Serves 4 to 6.

liguria roast chicken

schnitzel **parmigiano**

4 slices schnitzel-cut veal

2 eggs

2 tablespoons cornstarch

Toasted bread crumbs

$\frac{1}{2}$ cup vegetable oil

1 cup grated mozzarella cheese

4 slices boneless ham

**2 tablespoons grated parmesan
cheese**

TOMATO SAUCE

**1 (14- to 16-ounce) can tomato and
onion**

1 red bell pepper

1 tablespoon chopped fresh parsley

1 teaspoon dried basil

1 tablespoon tomato paste

Salt

Freshly ground black pepper

Cut veal into halves or into thirds. Roll
or pound until thin. Beat egg and
cornstarch together. Dip meat into
cornstarch mixture, then coat with bread
crumbs. Heat oil in a large skillet. Add
meat and cook on both sides until
golden. Drain on paper towels. Place
meat in a baking dish. Top with
mozzarella, ham and tomato sauce.
Sprinkle with parmesan cheese. Bake at
350°F for 15 to 20 minutes, or until
golden.

TOMATO SAUCE

Place tomato and onion with juice in the
bowl of a food processor or blender.
Halve, seed and core bell pepper. Add
bell pepper to processor along with
parsley, basil, tomato paste, salt and
pepper. Process until smooth.

Serves 4 to 6.

schnitzel parmigiano

olive and herb
fish steaks

If you don't like olives, try substituting black grapes.

2 onions
2 cloves garlic
2 tablespoons vegetable oil
1½ cups pitted ripe (black) olives
1½ teaspoons dried marjoram
1½ cups white wine vinegar
Salt
Freshly ground black pepper
1 tablespoon vegetable oil
4 fish steaks
1 tablespoon chopped fresh basil or
parsley

Peel and slice onions. Crush and peel garlic and chop fine. Heat two tablespoons oil in a skillet. Add onions and garlic and cook until clear. Add olives, marjoram, vinegar, salt and pepper. Cook for 2 to 3 minutes. Heat one tablespoon oil in another skillet. Add fish steaks and cook until just cooked through. Cooking time will depend on type of fish and thickness of the steak. Serve fish topped with olive mixture and garnished with basil or parsley.

Serves 4.

chinese whitebait
fritters

If whitebait is unavailable in your area, cut a white-fleshed fish fillet into very thin strips.

1 clove garlic
2 cups whitebait (not more than
1¾ inches long)
2 eggs
2 tablespoons chopped fresh parsley
Salt
2 tablespoons vegetable oil

Crush and peel garlic and chop fine. Wash, drain and dry whitebait. Lightly beat eggs with a fork in a bowl large enough to hold all the ingredients. Stir in whitebait, garlic parsley and salt. Heat oil in a large skillet. Measuring about ½ cup batter per fritter, add batter to oil, a few fritters at a time. Cook fritters until golden, turning to cook other side. Serve immediately.

Serves 2 to 3.

quick fish stew

Don't be put off by a "stew." It is an awful word that conjures up terrible childhood memories of forced food. This is a delicious dish and so simple to make.

1 pound white-fleshed fish
8 ounces mixed shellfish, such as mussels, prawns, shrimps or scallops
2 onions
Salt
Black pepper
1 (14- to 16-ounce) can tomatoes in juice
½ cup white wine or lemon juice
1 teaspoon dried oregano
1 tablespoon chopped fresh parsley

Trim fish and shellfish. Cut large pieces into cubes. Peel and slice onions. Layer half of the fish, shellfish and onions in a greased flameproof baking dish or saucepan. Season with salt and pepper. Chop tomatoes and remove cores. Pour half of the tomatoes with their juice over mixture in dish. Repeat layers. Add wine, oregano and parsley. Cook, uncovered, over low heat for 25 to 30 minutes, stirring occasionally. Serve with crusty bread.

Serves 4 to 6.

quick fish stew (top left),
olive and herb fish steaks (bottom left)
and chinese whitebait fritters

lamb shanks with tomatoes and lentils

The Italians waste nothing when it comes to meat. Many innovative dishes have evolved from a "waste not" approach to cooking.

1 cup orange lentils
1 carrot
2 ribs celery
2 cloves garlic
6 lamb shanks
2 (14- to 16-ounce) cans chunky tomato and onion
2 bay leaves
1 teaspoon dried marjoram
1 teaspoon dried thyme
3 large sprigs fresh parsley
1 tablespoon chopped fresh parsley

Wash lentils and place in the bottom of a large baking dish. Peel carrot and cut into slices. Trim celery and cut into cubes. Crush and peel garlic and chop fine. Place carrot, celery and garlic on top of lentils. Top with lamb shanks. Pour tomato and onion with juice over lamb. Add bay leaves, marjoram, thyme and parsley sprigs. Press into liquid. Tightly cover and cook at 325°F for 2 to 2½ hours. Skim fat from surface. Mix well. Serve lentils topped with shanks and sauce. Sprinkle with chopped parsley.

Serves 6.

mushroom chicken with sun-dried tomatoes

If you don't have wine on hand to cook with, use chicken stock.

8 chicken pieces
2 tablespoons vegetable oil
1 onion
2 cloves garlic
6 ounces fresh button mushrooms
1 teaspoon dried mixed herbs
½ cup white wine
½ cup chicken stock
2 tablespoons all-purpose flour
½ cup milk
4 slices sun-dried tomatoes
1 tablespoon chopped fresh parsley

Remove skin from chicken. Heat oil in a large skillet. Add chicken and cook until brown on all sides. Remove from skillet. Peel and chop onion. Crush, peel and chop garlic. Add onion and garlic to skillet and cook until onion is clear. Add mushrooms and herbs. Cook for 1 minute. Stir in wine and chicken stock. Bring to the boil. Mix flour and a little of the milk to make a smooth paste, then add remaining milk. Stir milk mixture into skillet. Cook, stirring, until sauce boils and thickens. Return chicken to skillet. Cook for 10 to 15 minutes. Garnish with sun-dried tomatoes and parsley.

Serves 4 to 6.

parmesan and pesto lamb cutlets

Used toasted or soft bread crumbs for this recipe – whatever you have on hand. Make soft bread crumbs out of stale bread and store them in the freezer.

1 egg
2 tablespoons pesto
2 tablespoons cornstarch
10 to 12 lamb cutlets
About ½ cup soft or toasted bread crumbs
¼ cup grated parmesan cheese
2 tablespoons vegetable oil

Beat egg, pesto and cornstarch together until combined. Dip cutlets in egg mixture to coat. Mix bread crumbs and parmesan cheese together. Coat cutlets with bread crumb mixture. Heat oil in a roasting pan. Place cutlets in oil and turn to coat. Bake at 375°F for 5 to 10 minutes, turning once during cooking, until cutlets are cooked. Or, shallow-fry cutlets in hot oil.

Serves 4 to 6.

lamb shanks with tomatoes and lentils (top left), parmesan and pesto lamb cutlets (bottom) and mushroom chicken with sun-dried tomatoes

veal marsala

Season flour with salt and pepper. Herbs or cheese can be added if wished.

4 ounces fresh button mushrooms
6 slices schnitzel-cut veal
1/2 cup all-purpose flour, seasoned to taste
2 tablespoons butter
2 tablespoons vegetable oil
1/2 cup marsala or sweet sherry
1/4 cup beef stock

Wash mushrooms and slice thin. Cut veal into halves or thirds to make small pieces. Coat veal in seasoned flour. Heat butter and oil in a skillet. Add meat and cook on both sides for 2 to 3 minutes, or until cooked. Drain on paper towels. Add mushrooms and cook for 2 to 3 minutes. Remove from pan and set aside. Pour off any remaining butter and oil in pan. Add marsala and beef stock to pan. Bring to the boil, scraping any sediment loose from bottom of pan. Return meat to pan. Cook for 5 minutes. Remove meat to a serving plate. Return mushrooms to pan. Bring to the boil. Pour sauce over meat and serve.

Serves 4 to 6.

tuscan roast

Sunday lunch is special in Italy. I was served a mixed roast in a Tuscan restaurant. It consisted of pigeon, rabbit and chicken and tasted wonderful. If you have access to food like rabbit, try a mixed roast, but most of us will have to settle for chicken.

6 to 8 chicken pieces
2 cloves garlic
1/4 cup vegetable oil
1 tablespoon dried rosemary

Remove skin and fat from chicken pieces. Crush and peel garlic and chop fine. Coat chicken with oil and sprinkle with rosemary and garlic. Roast at 375°F for 30 minutes, or until chicken is cooked. Transfer to a serving plate and serve with roast vegetables and steamed greens.

Serves 4 to 6.

tuscan beef stew

Try cooking this in a slow cooker if you have one, but reduce the amount of wine to 1/2 cup.

2 cloves garlic
1 onion
1 pound topside or chuck beef steak
3 tablespoons vegetable oil
1 1/2 teaspoons dried rosemary
1/4 teaspoon ground allspice
1/2 teaspoon ground cinnamon
1/4 cup tomato paste
3/4 cup dry red wine
Salt
Freshly ground black pepper

Crush, peel and chop garlic. Peel and finely chop onion. Trim fat from meat and cut meat into 1- to 1 1/2-inch cubes. Heat oil in a saucepan. Add garlic and onion and cook until onion is clear. Add rosemary and cook for 30 seconds. Add meat and brown. Stir in allspice, cinnamon, tomato paste, wine, salt and pepper. Cover and cook over low heat for 1 hour, or until meat is tender. Remove lid for the last 15 minutes of cooking.

Serves 4.

from top left: tuscan beef stew, veal marsala and tuscan roast

sausages italian style

1 pound precooked pork sausages
1 tablespoon vegetable oil
1 tablespoon all-purpose flour
1/4 cup lemon juice
1/4 cup white wine vinegar
1/2 cup beef stock
3 bay leaves
1/2 teaspoon ground sage
Freshly ground black pepper

Cut sausages into thirds. Heat oil in a large saucepan. Fry sausages in oil until browned. Stir in flour, then add lemon juice, vinegar, beef stock, bay leaves and sage. Cook, stirring, until sauce boils and thickens. Reduce heat and simmer for 5 minutes, stirring frequently. Remove bay leaves and add pepper.

Serves 4.

veal escalopes
with ham and cheese

6 medium slices schnitzel-cut veal
1 egg
2 tablespoons cornstarch
2 1/2 cups soft bread crumbs
1/2 cup vegetable oil, divided
12 slices prosciutto or ham
1 cup grated mozzarella cheese
1/2 cup grated parmesan cheese

Cut veal slices in half to make small pieces of meat. Cover with plastic wrap and roll with a rolling pin or use a meat mallet to flatten meat. Lightly beat egg and cornstarch together. Dip meat pieces in cornstarch mixture, then coat with bread crumbs. Heat two tablespoons of oil in a large skillet. Add meat and fry until golden on both sides. Repeat until all meat is cooked. Place cooked meat in a shallow baking dish. Cover with prosciutto or ham and sprinkle with cheeses. Broil for 2 to 3 minutes, or until cheese melts.

Serves 4 to 6.

sausages italian style
(top) and veal escalopes
with ham and cheese

polpettone

This is really the Italian version of a meat loaf.

2 slices bacon
2 slices bread
¼ cup milk
2 cloves garlic
16 to 18 ounces lean ground pork
1 egg
¼ teaspoon ground nutmeg
1 teaspoon dried marjoram
2 hard-cooked eggs, peeled
3 chipolatas (small Italian pork sausages)

Cut bacon into small pieces. Remove crusts from bread. Soak bread in milk for 5 minutes. Crush, peel and chop garlic. Place ground pork, bacon, bread-milk mixture, garlic, egg, nutmeg and marjoram in a bowl. Mix well. Turn mixture out onto a lightly floured surface and shape into an 8 x 4-inch rectangle. Place hard-cooked eggs and chipolatas down center of meat. Roll meat around filling. Place loaf in an oiled roasting pan and bake at 350°F for 1 hour, or until cooked. Serve with canned Italian tomatoes as a sauce if wished.

Serves 4 to 6.

oven-roasted lamb

1 (2- to 3-pound) piece lamb
4 potatoes
4 tomatoes
1 tablespoon vegetable oil
2 teaspoons dried oregano
Freshly ground black pepper

Trim fat from lamb. Cut lamb into cubes. Peel and cube potatoes. Cut tomatoes into quarters. Heat oil in a roasting pan until very hot. Add lamb and bake at 425°F for 5 minutes. Remove lamb from pan. Add potatoes to pan, tossing to coat with pan juices. Bake at 425°F for 5 minutes. Remove pan from oven and add lamb, tomatoes, oregano and pepper. Toss to coat, taking care not to break up tomatoes. Reduce oven temperate to 350°F and bake for 45 to 50 minutes, or until meat and potatoes are cooked.

Serves 4 to 6.

**polpettone and
oven-roasted lamb**

across the vines albanian
lamb casserole

Recipe ideas are often exchanged when people chat while performing menial tasks. During a wonderful day of grape-picking in a friend's vineyard, this recipe idea was shared.

2$\frac{1}{4}$ pounds lamb shoulder steaks

2 cups water

2 carrots

1 large parsnip

4 ribs celery

2 teaspoons black peppercorns

5 to 7 bay leaves, divided

TOPPING

3 eggs

2 tablespoons all-purpose flour

1 cup plain yogurt

$\frac{1}{2}$ teaspoon salt

Place meat in a medium saucepan. Add water and bring to the boil, skimming off scum that forms. Peel carrots and parsnip and trim celery. When water is clear of scum, add vegetables, peppercorns and one bay leaf. Cover and simmer gently for 1$\frac{1}{2}$ hours, or until meat is cooked. Cut meat into cubes and place in four or six ovenproof bowls. Strain stock, discarding vegetables. Let stock stand until lukewarm. Measure 1$\frac{1}{2}$ cups stock and reserve for topping. Pour topping over meat. Place a bay leaf on top of each dish. Bake at 350°F for 20 minutes, or until topping is lightly set.

TOPPING

Lightly beat eggs. Beat in flour, yogurt, salt and the reserved 1$\frac{1}{2}$ cups stock.

Serves 4 to 6.

across the vines albanian lamb casserole, chargrilled lamb fillets with creamy yogurt risotto

chargrilled
lamb fillets with
creamy yogurt risotto

RISOTTO

1 onion

2 cloves garlic

2 tablespoons butter

1 cup arborio rice

4 cups chicken stock, divided

Salt

$\frac{1}{2}$ cup plain yogurt

1 red bell pepper, roasted

Fresh herbs

LAMB FILLETS

6 lamb fillets

Vegetable oil

YOGURT SAUCE

$\frac{1}{2}$ cup plain yogurt

1 tablespoon red wine or balsamic vinegar

1 tablespoon chopped fresh parsley

RISOTTO

Peel onion and chop fine. Crush and peel garlic and chop fine. Melt butter in a large skillet. Add onion and garlic and cook for 5 minutes, or until clear. Add rice and cook until clear and coated with butter. Add one cup of chicken stock and stir until liquid has evaporated. Add remaining stock, $\frac{1}{2}$ cup at a time, and continue to cook, stirring, until rice is cooked and stock has evaporated. Season with salt. Stir in yogurt. Cut bell pepper into thin strips and stir into risotto. To serve, place a round of risotto in the center of each of four hot serving plates. Arrange lamb in a stack over risotto. Serve with Yogurt Sauce and garnish with fresh herbs.

LAMB FILLETS

Brush lamb with oil. Cook lamb in a skillet, under a broiler or on the grill for 2 to 3 minutes, or until just cooked.

YOGURT SAUCE

Mix yogurt, vinegar and parsley together.

Serves 4.

mussel soup

30 fresh mussels in the shell
2 cloves garlic
2 onions
2 tablespoons vegetable oil
2 teaspoons chili paste
1 cup dry white wine
1 cup fish stock
2 (14- to 16-ounce) cans tomatoes in
    juice
2 tablespoons chopped fresh parsley
Salt
Freshly ground black pepper

Scrub mussels and debeard. Crush and
peel garlic and chop fine. Peel onions
and chop fine. Heat oil in a large
saucepan. Add onion and garlic and cook
for 5 minutes over medium heat. Add
chili, wine, fish stock and tomatoes with
their juice. Bring to the boil. Add mussels
and cook, covered, over medium heat for
5 minutes, or until mussels open. Discard
any that do not open. Reserve 8 to 12
mussels for garnish, removing and
discarding top shell. Remove remaining
mussels from shells. Cut mussels in half
and return to tomato mixture. Bring to
the boil. Add parsley and season with salt
and pepper. Serve hot. Garnish with
reserved mussels.

Serves 4 to 6.

mussel soup, mussel fritters and
grilled mussels with fresh herbs

mussel fritters

15 fresh mussels in the shell
2 eggs
2 tablespoons cornstarch
1 teaspoon baking powder
1/2 teaspoon salt
Freshly ground black pepper
1 tablespoon lemon juice
1/4 cup chopped green onions (green
    part only)
2 tablespoons vegetable oil
Lemon wedges

Scrub mussels and debeard. Place in a
saucepan over medium heat and cook for
about 5 minutes, or until shells open.
Discard any that do not open. Remove
mussels from shells and coarsely chop.
Beat eggs. Add cornstarch, baking
powder, salt, pepper, lemon juice, green
onions and chopped mussels. Heat oil in
a skillet or on a griddle. Measuring about
1/4 cup batter per fritter, add batter to
the skillet, a few fritters at a time. Cook
until golden on both sides. Serve with
lemon wedges.

Makes 6.

grilled mussels with fresh herbs

About 48 fresh mussels in the shells
About 8 big stalks fresh rosemary
1/4 cup lemon juice
2 tablespoons chopped fresh mixed
    herbs, such as parsley, chives,
    thyme or rosemary

Scrub mussels and debeard. Place a layer
of rosemary on the cooking rack of a
preheated grill. Place mussels on top of
rosemary and arrange another layer of
rosemary over mussels. Cook over hot
coals until mussels open. Discard any
mussels that do not open. Break off top
shell. Arrange mussels on a platter. Pour
lemon juice over mussels and sprinkle
with chopped herbs.

Serves 4 to 6.

mediterranean **lamb cutlets** with white bean medley

The pesto used in this recipe is available in jars at the supermarket or specialty food store. Use any other flavored pesto if preferred.

1 egg

2 tablespoons roasted bell pepper pesto

2 tablespoons cornstarch

12 lamb cutlets

About $1/2$ cup soft or toasted bread crumbs

2 tablespoons vegetable oil

WHITE BEAN MEDLEY

1 (15- to 16-ounce) can cannellini-style butter beans

2 tomatoes

$1/4$ cup torn basil leaves

2 tablespoons vinaigrette

Beat egg, pesto and cornstarch together until combined. Dip cutlets into egg mixture to coat. Cover cutlets with bread crumbs, pressing crumbs on. Heat oil in a roasting pan. Place cutlets in pan, turning to coat. Bake at 375°F for 5 to 10 minutes, or until preferred degree of doneness. Serve with White Bean Medley.

WHITE BEAN MEDLEY

Drain beans. Cut tomatoes into $1/4$-inch cubes. Mix beans, tomatoes, basil and vinaigrette together.

Serves 4.

mediterranean lamb cutlets with white bean medley and country kitchen tomato tart

country kitchen
tomato tart

2 sheets savory short crust pastry
1 (15- to 16-ounce) can whole-kernel corn
1 (8-ounce) carton sour cream
4 eggs
1 teaspoon chili paste
3 tablespoons chopped fresh parsley
3 medium tomatoes
¼ cup basil pesto
½ cup grated mozzarella cheese

Line four 5-inch tart pans or small pie plates with pastry. Bake blind at 400°F for 10 minutes. Remove baking blind material. Drain corn. Mix sour cream and eggs together until combined. Add corn, chili and parsley. Divide mixture among pastry shells. Cut tomatoes into thick slices. Arrange tomato slices over corn mixture in each pan. Bake at 400°F for 5 minutes, then reduce oven temperature to 325°F and cook for 15 to 20 minutes, or until tarts are set. Top tomatoes with basil pesto and sprinkle with grated cheese. Broil until golden. Serve with a green salad.

Serves 4.

vegetables

Eat vegetables first with your eyes, letting the wonderful colors and shapes inspire you to create some memorable tastes. Keep it simple but make your vegetable cookery classy. The more you do with vegetables, the more you'll want to do.

ratatouille and
bacon stack

*Impressive-looking food is often stacked or
piled onto a plate rather than being set out.
This makes a great meal. Use red, green or
yellow bell peppers or a mixture of all. Add
one-fourth cup dry red wine to this if wished,
but you will need to cook the mixture longer.*

2 large eggplants

Salt

3 onions

3 cloves garlic

8 tomatoes

2 tablespoons vegetable oil

1 bay leaf

1 teaspoon dried rosemary

1 teaspoon dried basil

$1/2$ teaspoon salt

Freshly ground black pepper

8 slices bacon

3 bell peppers

4 zucchini

$1/4$ cup vegetable oil

1 (7.5-ounce) can salmon, drained
   and flaked

Wash eggplants, trim ends and cut into
$1/2$-inch-wide rounds. Sprinkle a paper
towel with salt and arrange eggplant on
towel. Sprinkle top of slices with salt. Set
aside while preparing rest of dish. Peel
onions and slice. Crush, peel and chop
garlic. Cut tomatoes in half and remove
stem end. Heat two tablespoons oil in a
saucepan. Add onion and garlic and cook
for 5 minutes, or until clear. Add
tomatoes, bay leaf, rosemary and basil.
Cook, uncovered, for 15 minutes, or until
thick. Season with salt and pepper.
Remove and discard bay leaf. Cut bacon
slices lengthwise into thin strips. Cut bell
peppers into quarters, removing core and
seeds. Trim zucchini and cut lengthwise
into thirds. Wash salt from eggplant and
wipe slices dry. Brush eggplant, bell
peppers and zucchini with $1/4$ cup oil.
Broil eggplant, bell peppers, zucchini and
bacon until golden. To serve, layer
broiled vegetables with tomato mixture,
bacon and salmon on individual plates.
Serve with crusty bread and a green
salad.

Serves 4.

ratatouille and bacon stack

ratatouille

Anyone who has discovered this delicious vegetable combination has his or her own special blend. This is mine. Feel free to experiment with your own brew depending on what is in season at the right price.

1 eggplant
Salt
1 onion
3 cloves garlic
1 tablespoon vegetable oil
1 tablespoon tomato paste
4 tomatoes
1 red bell pepper
1 green bell pepper
4 zucchini
1 teaspoon dried rosemary
$^1/_2$ teaspoon dried thyme
1 bay leaf
1 tablespoon chopped fresh parsley

Trim ends from eggplant. Cut into slices and sprinkle with salt. Set aside while preparing remaining ingredients. Peel and finely chop onion. Crush, peel and chop garlic. Heat oil in a skillet or flameproof baking dish. Add onion and garlic and cook for 3 to 5 minutes, or until onion is clear. Mix onion, garlic and tomato paste together in the baking dish. Dice tomatoes. Seed and slice red and green bell peppers. Trim zucchini and cut into $^1/_2$-inch slices. Add tomatoes, bell peppers, zucchini, rosemary, thyme and bay leaf to baking dish. Wash salt from eggplant and cut each slice into quarters. Add to baking dish. Mix gently. Cover and bake at 350°F for 1 to 1$^1/_4$ hours. Sprinkle with chopped parsley and serve.

Serves 4 to 6.

sage butter **zucchini**

6 zucchini
2 tablespoons butter
2 tablespoons chopped fresh sage or
**   2 teaspoons dried**
2 tablespoons grated parmesan
**   cheese**
2 tablespoons pine nuts, toasted
Salt
Freshly ground black pepper

Trim zucchini. Cut into 1-inch pieces and steam or microwave until just cooked. Drain well. Place in a serving dish. Heat butter in a small saucepan. Add sage and cook until butter browns. Sprinkle parmesan cheese and pine nuts over zucchini. Season with salt and pepper. Pour butter over zucchini and serve immediately.

Serves 4.

herb's **carrots**

4 medium carrots
3 cloves garlic
2 tablespoons olive oil
1/2 cup white wine vinegar
1 tablespoon chopped fresh oregano
**   or marjoram or 1 teaspoon dried**
1/2 teaspoon freshly crushed chili
**   pepper**
1/2 teaspoon granulated sugar
Salt
Freshly ground black pepper

Peel carrots and cut into 1/4-inch rounds. Cook carrots in boiling salted water for 5 minutes. Drain well. Crush, peel and sliver garlic. Heat oil in a large skillet. Add garlic and carrots and cook for 2 minutes, stirring frequently. Add vinegar, oregano or marjoram, chili, sugar, salt and pepper and cook for about 10 minutes, or until all liquid has evaporated. Serve warm or at room temperature.

Serves 4.

sage butter zucchini and herb's carrots

brussels sprouts
with almond pesto

When my children were little, I used to try to persuade them to eat brussels sprouts by telling them they were fairy cabbages. Of course it didn't work as these strong-flavored vegetables overpower the appeal of fantasy. This is a delicious way to serve brussels sprouts. If you don't have time to make your own pesto, ready-made pesto will do just as well.

1 pound brussels sprouts
¹/₄ cup Almond Pesto
¹/₄ cup flaked almonds, toasted

Wash and trim brussels sprouts. Cut a cross in the stem end of each sprout. Steam, boil or microwave sprouts until just tender. Drain well. Toss sprouts with Almond Pesto and garnish with almonds.

ALMOND PESTO

³/₄ cup tightly packed fresh basil leaves
1 clove garlic
Pinch salt
¹/₄ cup olive oil, divided
¹/₂ cup almonds, toasted
2 tablespoons grated parmesan cheese

Place basil in the bowl of a food processor or in a mortar. Crush and peel garlic. Add garlic to basil along with salt and half of the oil. Process, or pound with a pestle, to a smooth paste. Add almonds and remaining oil and process or pound until nuts are lightly chopped. Mix in parmesan cheese.

Makes ³/₄ cup.

zucchini and **mint molds** with fresh tomato sauce

If mint is not available, use fresh basil.

6 zucchini
1 tablespoon salt
1 tablespoon chopped fresh mint
    leaves
1 tablespoon chopped fresh chives or
    green onions (green part only)
Freshly ground black pepper
1 tomato
Fresh Tomato Sauce

Trim zucchini and coarsely grate. Place in a sieve and stir in salt. Let drain for 30 minutes to 1 hour. Squeeze zucchini, then mix with mint, chives and pepper. Cut tomato in half and remove seeds. Cut into $1/4$-inch dice. Stir into zucchini mixture. Pack zucchini mixture into six small ramekins. Refrigerate until ready to serve. Serve with Fresh Tomato Sauce.

Serves 4.

FRESH TOMATO SAUCE
6 tomatoes
1 onion
2 cloves garlic
1 tablespoon vegetable oil
$1/4$ cup chopped fresh basil leaves

Cut tomatoes in half and remove core. Coarsely chop. Peel onion and chop fine. Crush, peel and chop garlic. Heat oil in a saucepan. Add onion and garlic and cook for 5 minutes, or until clear not colored. Add tomatoes and basil and cook for 5 minutes, breaking tomatoes up with a wooden spoon. Leave chunky or puree in a sieve or blender. Serve warm or cold.

brussels sprouts with almond pesto, zucchini and mint molds with fresh tomato sauce

fresh **vegetable**
frittata

Frittata has long been a standby for a quick meal in our home. It always provided the opportunity to feed vegetables to my toddlers on those trying days when they wouldn't eat "what's good for them."

1 pound fresh vegetables, such as carrots, bell peppers, potatoes, broccoli or leeks

2 tablespoons vegetable oil

4 eggs

Salt

Freshly ground black pepper

Shaved parmesan cheese

Trim vegetables and cut into small pieces. Peel vegetables if necessary and grate vegetables such as carrots and potatoes. Heat oil in a large skillet. Add vegetables and cook until vegetables start to wilt. Beat eggs with salt. Pour egg mixture over vegetables in skillet. Cook frittata until lightly browned. Turn and cook other side. Sprinkle with pepper and parmesan cheese. Cut into wedges to serve.

Serves 4 to 6.

baked **frittata** cake

4 medium carrots

6 large zucchini

2 onions

6 eggs

$\frac{1}{2}$ cup all-purpose flour

1 teaspoon baking powder

Salt

Black pepper

1 teaspoon curry powder

Scrub or peel carrots. Wash and trim zucchini. Peel onions. Grate carrots, zucchini and onions. Place in a sieve and let stand for 30 minutes. Squeeze out moisture from vegetables. Place vegetables in a bowl. Add eggs and mix until combined. Sift flour and baking powder into vegetable mixture. Add salt, pepper and curry powder. Mix until combined and smooth. Pour into a deep 9-inch pie plate lined with parchment or waxed paper. Bake at 350ºF for 40 to 45 minutes, or until golden and set. Cut into wedges to serve.

Serves 4 to 6.

baked frittata cake and fresh vegetable frittata

potato layer bake

6 to 8 medium potatoes
1 clove garlic
³/₄ cup milk
¹/₄ teaspoon ground nutmeg
Salt
Black pepper
1 cup grated gruyere cheese

Peel potatoes and slice thin. Crush and peel garlic. Rub garlic over bottom and sides of a greased shallow baking dish. Arrange potato slices in dish. Mix milk and nutmeg together. Season with salt and pepper. Pour milk mixture over potatoes. Top with grated cheese. Cover and bake at 350°F for 40 to 45 minutes, or until potatoes are tender. Remove lid and broil cheese until golden. Cut into wedges to serve.

Serves 4 to 6.

potato and apple bake

4 medium onions
4 medium potatoes
4 medium apples
1 (1¹/₄-ounce) envelope dry chicken soup mix
2 cups water
¹/₂ teaspoon salt
1 tablespoon finely chopped fresh sage or 2 teaspoons dried
3 tablespoons butter

Peel onions and potatoes. Core apples with an apple corer. Cut onions, potatoes and apples into ¹/₄-inch-thick slices. Place layers of onion, potato and apple in a greased 13 x 9-inch baking dish. Mix chicken soup mix with water and salt. Pour soup mixture over potato mixture. Sprinkle with sage and dot with butter. Cover with a lid or foil and bake at 400°F for 45 minutes. Remove lid and cook for 10 minutes.

Serves 6.

potato and olive pie

This is delicious served as an accompaniment or as a light meal.

Melted butter
¹/₂ cup toasted bread crumbs
4 cups unseasoned mashed cooked potatoes
¹/₄ cup sun-dried tomato pesto
8 slices prosciutto or ham
1 cup pitted ripe (black) olives
1 cup grated sharp cheddar cheese
¹/₄ cup torn basil leaves

Liberally grease a loose-bottom 8-inch cake pan or springform pan with melted butter. Place bread crumbs in pan and toss to coat inside of pan. Spread half of the mashed potatoes in the bottom of the pan. Spread pesto over potatoes, then place prosciutto or ham over pesto. Top with a layer of olives. Spread remaining mashed potatoes on top. Sprinkle with grated cheese. Bake at 400°F for 30 minutes, or until heated through. Garnish with basil and cut into wedges to serve.

Serves 4 to 6.

potato layer bake, potato and apple bake and potato and olive pie

italian **baked** potatoes

6 medium potatoes
1 (14- to 16-ounce) can tomatoes in
**   juice**
2 cups grated mozzarella cheese
2 tablespoons chopped fresh basil
**   or 1 tablespoon dried**
$^1\!/_2$ cup grated parmesan cheese
3 tablespoons olive oil, divided
$^1\!/_2$ cup soft bread crumbs

Peel potatoes and cook in boiling salted
water for 10 minutes. Drain well. Let
cool, then cut into $^1\!/_2$-inch slices. Arrange
half of the potatoes in the bottom of a
greased shallow baking dish. Top with
half of the tomatoes. Sprinkle with half
of the mozzarella cheese, half of the
basil and half of the parmesan cheese.
Pour one tablespoon of oil on top.
Repeat layers. Sprinkle with bread
crumbs and remaining two tablespoons
oil. Bake at 375°F for 30 minutes, or until
potatoes are cooked and top is golden
brown.

Serves 4 to 6.

italian baked potatoes,
italian potato salad and
tuscan potatoes

tuscan potatoes

These potatoes are the sort of thing you develop a reputation on. They are simple, great tasting and put a modern slant on roast potatoes.

6 medium potatoes
4 cloves garlic
¼ cup olive oil
1½ teaspoons dried rosemary
Freshly ground black pepper

Peel potatoes and cut into 1-inch cubes. Crush and peel garlic and chop fine. Heat oil in a roasting pan. Add potatoes, garlic and rosemary. Bake at 375°F for 30 to 40 minutes, or until potatoes are cooked, turning potatoes frequently during cooking. Arrange on a serving plate and season with pepper.

Serves 4.

italian potato salad

Prosciutto can be used instead of bacon and roasted bell peppers can replace the pickled ones. Add some sun-dried tomatoes, too, if wished.

6 medium potatoes
4 slices bacon
1 cup ripe (black) olives
½ cup drained pickled bell peppers
¼ cup fresh basil leaves
½ cup vinaigrette

Peel potatoes and cut into thick slices. Cook in boiling salted water until tender. Drain well. Let cool. Cut bacon into thin strips and cook for 3 to 5 minutes, or until lightly browned. Place potatoes, olives, bell peppers, basil and bacon in a bowl. Carefully stir in vinaigrette.

Serves 4 to 5.

quick calzone

Use grated cheddar or colby cheese instead of parmesan if preferred.

2 large pita (pocket) breads
4 zucchini
2 red bell peppers
8 to 10 fresh mushrooms
Vegetable oil
1 tablespoon capers
2 tablespoons sun-dried tomato
   pesto
2 tablespoons grated parmesan
   cheese

Cut through top layer of each pita bread through the center from edge to edge. Turn and cut at right angles to the first cut. Trim zucchini. Cut in half lengthwise, then into $1\frac{1}{2}$-inch chunks. Core bell peppers and cut into eighths. Wipe mushrooms and cut in half, if large. Place vegetables in a baking pan and brush with oil. Broil vegetables until zucchini are lightly golden and bell pepper skins blistered. Place vegetables in a bowl and stir in capers and pesto. Carefully open pita breads along the cuts and fill with vegetable mixture. Brush cut top of pitas with oil and sprinkle with parmesan cheese. Bake at 400°F for 10 minutes, or until heated through. Cut into wedges to serve.

Serves 4 to 6.

quick calzone

green bean salad

Green beans aren't my favorite vegetable. They are something to be suffered! Try them in this salad – they take on a whole new perspective.

1 pound fresh green beans
2 slices bacon
1 red onion
¼ cup chopped fresh chives
2 tablespoons chopped fresh sage
3 tablespoons white vinegar
¼ cup olive oil
Salt
Freshly ground black pepper

Break off ends of beans. Cut beans in half if they are long. Cook in boiling water for 10 minutes, or until just tender. Drain and refresh under cold water. Drain well. Finely chop bacon. Cook bacon in a skillet for 5 minutes. Peel onion and cut into rings. Add onion rings to skillet and cook until soft. Place beans, bacon, onion, chives and sage in a bowl. Add vinegar and oil to skillet bacon was cooked in. Stir to loosen cooking sediment. Season with salt and pepper and pour over bean mixture. Toss salad and serve.

Serves 4.

roasted vegetable salad

Don't be limited by the vegetables used in this recipe. Use whatever you have on hand or whatever is in season.

2 cloves garlic
¼ cup olive oil
8 asparagus spears
3 zucchini
1 red bell pepper
6 fresh mushrooms
¼ cup chopped fresh basil leaves

Crush and peel garlic and chop fine. Mix garlic with oil and pour into a roasting pan. Snap ends off asparagus. Cut zucchini lengthwise into quarters. Seed bell pepper and cut into thin strips. Cut mushrooms in half. Place vegetables in roasting pan and toss with oil. Roast at 400°F for 15 minutes, or until vegetables start to brown. Remove from oven and let cool. Toss with basil and serve warm.

Serves 4 to 6.

green bean salad, roasted vegetable salad and pickled eggplant salad

pickled eggplant
salad

This is a superb salad which is always enjoyed. It's a little fiddly but worth the effort.

2 medium eggplant
Salt
Vegetable oil
4 cloves garlic
1 red bell pepper
1 cup chopped fresh parsley
1 cup ripe (black) olives
1 cup white vinegar
1 cup water
1 teaspoon salt
$1/2$ teaspoon freshly ground black pepper
$1/4$ teaspoon ground red (cayenne) pepper

Cut eggplant into $1/2$-inch slices. Sprinkle cut sides with salt and let stand for 30 minutes. Wash salt from eggplant and dry slices on paper towels. Heat oil in a skillet. Add eggplant and cook until lightly brown on each side. Drain on paper towels. Crush and peel garlic. Cut into thin pieces. Seed and slice bell pepper. Layer eggplant, garlic, bell pepper, parsley and olives in a non-metallic dish. Heat vinegar, water, salt, black pepper and red pepper together until boiling. Remove from heat and pour over layered eggplant mixture. Make sure all the eggplant is covered. Cover dish and refrigerate for several hours before serving.

Serves 4.

pumpkin cubed salad

1 (1-pound) pumpkin
12 ounces conchiglie
1 tablespoon vegetable oil
4 ounces fresh snow peas
1 cup roasted peanuts
1/2 cup vinaigrette
Shaved parmesan cheese
Snow pea sprouts

Peel pumpkin. Cut into even-sized pieces and cook in boiling salted water for 15 to 20 minutes, or until tender. Drain and cut into 1-inch cubes. Cook pasta in boiling salted water for 8 to 10 minutes, or until tender. Drain and toss with oil. Let cool. Trim snow peas. Blanch in boiling water for 3 minutes, then drain. Mix pumpkin, pasta, snow peas and peanuts together. Just before serving, toss with vinaigrette. Garnish with parmesan cheese and snow pea sprouts.

Serves 4 to 6.

pasta bean salad

12 ounces fusilli
1 tablespoon vegetable oil
1 cup frozen broad (fava) beans
1/2 cup vinaigrette
1 teaspoon dried sage
1 red bell pepper
1/4 cup chopped fresh chives

Cook pasta in boiling salted water for 8 to 10 minutes, or until tender. Drain and toss with oil. Let cool. Cook beans in boiling water for 3 to 5 minutes, or until tender. Drain well and shell if wished. Mix beans, pasta and vinaigrette together. Sprinkle with sage. Core and slice red bell pepper. Add bell pepper to pasta mixture along with chives. Toss well.

Serves 4 to 6.

from back left clockwise: guacamole pasta salad, pumpkin cubed salad, mother's italian salad and pasta bean salad

mother's italian salad

12 ounces macaroni
1 tablespoon vegetable oil
6 slices pastrami
½ cup pine nuts, toasted
½ cup pimiento-stuffed green olives
Freshly ground black pepper
¼ cup basil pesto
½ cup mayonnaise

Cook pasta in boiling water for 8 to 10 minutes, or until tender. Drain and toss with oil. Let cool. Cut pastrami into thin strips. Mix pasta, pastrami, pine nuts and olives together. Season with pepper. Mix pesto and mayonnaise together and serve with pasta mixture.

Serves 4.

guacamole pasta salad

12 ounces fusilli
1 tablespoon vegetable oil
4 tomatoes
1 clove garlic
2 ripe avocados
¼ cup lemon juice
¼ teaspoon chili powder
¼ teaspoon salt
1 tablespoon sour cream
Paprika

Cook pasta in boiling salted water for 8 to 10 minutes, or until tender. Drain and toss with oil. Remove core from tomatoes and cut into cubes. Crush, peel and chop garlic. Peel and pit one avocado and mash with lemon juice, chili powder, salt and garlic to make guacamole. Peel and pit second avocado; cut into cubes. Toss pasta, tomato cubes and avocado cubes together. Pile guacamole on top of pasta. Garnish with sour cream and paprika.

Serves 4.

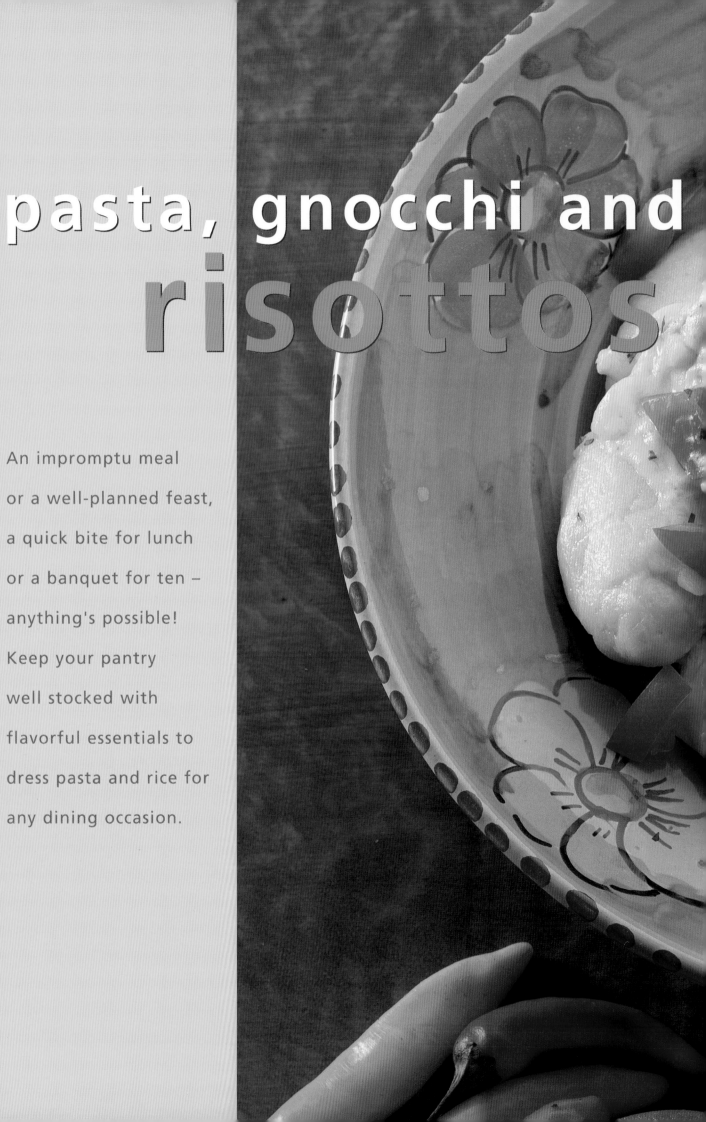

pasta, gnocchi and risottos

An impromptu meal
or a well-planned feast,
a quick bite for lunch
or a banquet for ten –
anything's possible!
Keep your pantry
well stocked with
flavorful essentials to
dress pasta and rice for
any dining occasion.

potato gnocchi
with spicy chicken sauce

GNOCCHI

1 pound potatoes

2 tablespoons butter

1 egg

Salt

Freshly ground black pepper

1¼ to 1½ cups all-purpose flour

SPICY CHICKEN SAUCE

8 ounces boned and skinned chicken
meat, such as tenderloins

1 onion

¼ cup (½ stick) butter or margarine

½ teaspoon curry powder

½ teaspoon chili powder

3 tablespoons all-purpose flour

2 cups milk

1 tomato

GNOCCHI

Peel potatoes, cut into even-sized pieces and cook in boiling salted water for 15 to 20 minutes, or until tender. Mash potatoes and add butter, egg, salt, pepper and enough flour to make a soft manageable dough. Do this in the food processor if wished. Measure tablespoons of mixture and shape into ovals. Place a few gnocchi at a time in boiling water and simmer for 1 to 2 minutes, or until gnocchi rise to the top. Remove with a slotted spoon, draining well. Place in a serving dish. Pour Spicy Chicken Sauce over gnocchi. Garnish with tomato.

SPICY CHICKEN SAUCE

Cut chicken into thin strips. Peel onion and chop fine. Melt butter or margarine in a saucepan. Add onion and cook for 3 to 5 minutes, or until soft but not colored. Add curry powder and chili powder and cook for 30 seconds to 1 minute, or until spices smell fragrant. Stir in flour and cook for 1 minute. Remove from heat and gradually stir in milk. Cook until sauce boils and thickens. Add chicken and cook for 3 to 5 minutes, or until chicken is just cooked. Cut tomato in half. Remove seeds and cut into small cubes.

Serves 4.

potato gnocchi with spicy chicken sauce

gnocchi with tomato and basil sauce

Semolina is one of those products we don't use much of these days. It's a useful product to have in the pantry, especially when cooking Italian fare. You'll find it in the cereal or flour section of the supermarket.

2 cups milk

1/4 teaspoon salt

1/4 teaspoon freshly ground black pepper

1/4 teaspoon ground nutmeg

1/2 cup semolina

1/2 cup grated mozzarella cheese, divided

1/4 cup grated parmesan cheese, divided

2 egg yolks

2 tablespoons butter

1 tablespoon butter, melted

BASIL AND TOMATO SAUCE

1 (14- to 16-ounce) can tomatoes in juice

2 cloves garlic

1 1/2 teaspoons dried basil

1/4 teaspoon freshly ground black pepper

Pinch ground chilies

Put milk, salt, pepper and nutmeg in a saucepan. Heat gently. Sprinkle semolina over milk. Bring to the boil, then lower heat and simmer, stirring constantly, for 4 to 5 minutes, or until very thick. Remove from heat. Add half of the cheeses. Add egg yolks and two tablespoons butter. Beat to combine. Spread in a well-greased baking pan. Cover and let stand until cold. Cut into rounds using a 2-inch fluted cookie cutter. Arrange rounds on an ovenproof serving plate or dish. Brush tops with melted butter. Sprinkle with remaining cheeses. Broil until golden. Serve with Basil and Tomato Sauce.

BASIL AND TOMATO SAUCE

Put tomatoes with their juice in bowl of a food processor. Process until coarsely chopped. Crush, peel and mash garlic. In a saucepan, combine tomatoes, garlic, basil, pepper and ground chili. Gently heat through.

Serves 6.

quick lasagne

Every Italian family in every region of Italy has their own version of lasagne. The idea of layering sheets of pasta with other ingredients can be varied to give different flavors.

1 onion
1 clove garlic
1 rib celery
1 pound lean ground beef
1½ teaspoons dried basil
1 (15-ounce) can tomato sauce
Salt
Black pepper
1 (8-ounce) carton ricotta or cottage cheese
1 cup grated mozzarella cheese
¼ cup grated parmesan cheese
14 ounces fresh lasagne
1 (14- to 16-ounce) can seasoned tomatoes
¼ cup soft bread crumbs
1 tablespoon butter

Peel and chop onion. Crush, peel and chop garlic. Finely chop celery. Mix ground beef, basil, tomato sauce, onion, garlic, celery, salt and pepper together in a bowl. Mix ricotta, mozzarella and parmesan cheeses together. Place one-fourth of the meat mixture in a baking dish. Cover with a layer of lasagne, one-fourth of the tomatoes and one-fourth of the cheese mixture. Repeat layers until all ingredients are used. Sprinkle with bread crumbs and dot with butter. Bake at 375°F for 40 minutes.

Serves 4.

gnocchi with tomato and basil sauce and quick lasagne

tomato, mushroom and basil **risotto**

1 onion
¼ cup (½ stick) butter
2 cups arborio rice
4 cups beef stock, divided
1 (14- to 16-ounce) can tomatoes
1½ teaspoons dried basil
4 ounces fresh mushrooms
Shaved parmesan cheese

Peel onion and chop fine. Melt butter or margarine in large saucepan or deep skillet. Add onion and cook until clear. Add rice and cook until rice looks white. Add one cup of beef stock and cook risotto, uncovered, stirring often. Gradually add remaining beef stock as liquid is absorbed. Seed and core tomatoes, and cut into cubes. Add tomatoes and basil to risotto. Slice mushrooms thin. Cook risotto for 15 to 20 minutes. Five minutes before end of cooking time, add mushrooms. Serve garnished with parmesan cheese.

Serves 4 to 6.

polenta with mozzarella, **prosciutto** and tomato

POLENTA
1 cup yellow cornmeal
1 cup cold water
1½ cups boiling water
1½ teaspoons salt
1 clove garlic
1 tablespoon vegetable oil
TOPPING
8 slices mozzarella cheese
8 slices prosciutto
8 slices tomato
1 teaspoon dried basil

Mix cornmeal and cold water together in a saucepan. Stir in boiling water and salt. Cook, stirring, for 10 minutes. Continue to cook over low heat for 15 minutes or longer, stirring occasionally to prevent sticking. Spread polenta into an 8-inch square baking dish. Crush and peel garlic. Cut polenta into 8 squares. Brush polenta with oil, rub with garlic and broil on one side. Top each square with a slice of mozzarella cheese, a slice of prosciutto and a tomato slice. Sprinkle with basil. Broil for 1 minute. Serve immediately.

Serves 4.

spinach and potato **gnocchi**

Gnocchi can be made with semolina, potato or bread as its base. It is filling fare and needs to be served with light accompaniments or sauces. Serve as an entree or as part of a main course.

12 spinach leaves
1 pound potatoes
2 tablespoons butter
1 egg
Salt
Black pepper
1¼ to 1½ cups all-purpose flour
4 tablespoons butter
½ cup grated parmesan cheese

Wash spinach and cook for 3 to 4 minutes in the water clinging to leaves. Drain and squeeze water from spinach. Chop fine. Peel potatoes and cook in boiling salted water for 15 to 20 minutes, or until tender. Drain well. Mash potatoes and add two tablespoons butter, egg, salt, pepper and spinach. Add enough flour to make a stiff dough. Knead until smooth. For speed, this mashing and mixing can be done in a food processor. Using a measuring tablespoon, scoop spoonsful of mixture. Shape into ovals and place on a floured surface. Cook a few at a time in simmering water until they rise to the top. This takes 1 to 2 minutes. Remove with a slotted spoon. Arrange in a greased baking dish. Melt four tablespoons butter and pour over gnocchi. Sprinkle with parmesan cheese and broil until cheese browns slightly.

Serves 4 as an entree or accompaniment.

seafood risotto (top), tomato, mushroom and basil risotto (middle), spinach and potato gnocchi (bottom right), and polenta with mozzarella, prosciutto and tomato

seafood risotto

1 onion
1 carrot
2 ribs celery
¼ cup (½ stick) butter
2 cups arborio rice
½ cup dry white wine
4 cups chicken stock, divided
½ teaspoon dried thyme
2 cups cubed fish or a mixture of fish, such as scallops, mussels, prawns or white-fleshed fish

Peel onion and chop fine. Scrub carrot and cut into small cubes. Trim celery and dice. Melt butter in a large skillet. Add onion, carrot and celery and cook for 5 minutes. Add rice and cook for 2 to 3 minutes, or until rice turns white. Add wine, one cup of chicken stock and thyme. Stir well. Bring to the boil. Reduce heat and simmer, uncovered, for 15 to 20 minutes, or until cooked but firm to the bite, adding more stock as rice dries out. Five minutes before the end of cooking time, add fish and cook until fish is cooked through. Serve immediately.

Serves 4 to 6.

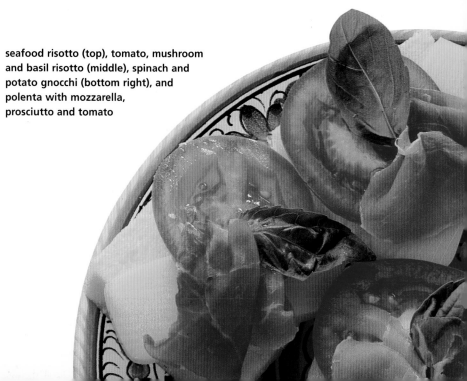

macaroni, salmon and
asparagus bake

2 cups macaroni
1 (7.5-ounce) can salmon
**1 (12- to 15-ounce) can asparagus
   spears**
4 tablespoons cornstarch
2$\frac{1}{2}$ cups milk
3 cups grated sharp cheddar cheese
Salt
Freshly ground black pepper

Cook macaroni in a large saucepan in
boiling salted water for 10 minutes, or
until tender. Drain and return to saucepan.
Drain salmon and remove bones. Drain
asparagus, reserving liquid. Mix cornstarch
with a little reserved asparagus liquid to
make a paste. Mix cornstarch mixture
with remaining asparagus liquid and milk.
Pour milk mixture over macaroni and
cook until sauce boils and thickens. Stir in
half the cheese and season with salt and
pepper. Spread half the macaroni mixture
in a baking dish. Arrange asparagus spears
and salmon on top. Spread remaining
macaroni mixture over salmon. Sprinkle
with remaining cheese. Broil until cheese
is golden and heated through.

Serves 4.

quick storecupboard
seafood lasagne

1 (7.5-ounce) can salmon

2 (4-ounce) cans shrimp

2 green onions

1 teaspoon grated lemon peel

1 tablespoon lemon juice

Freshly ground black pepper

**1 (14- to 16-ounce) jar creamy pasta
  sauce**

8 ounces lasagne

1 cup grated mozzarella cheese

Drain salmon and shrimp. Wash, trim and
slice green onions. Mix salmon, shrimp,
green onions, lemon peel, lemon juice,
pepper and pasta sauce together. Cook
lasagne in boiling water for 3 minutes.
Drain. Place a layer of lasagne on the
bottom of a greased 11 x 7-inch lasagne
dish. Top with one-fourth of the sauce
mixture. Repeat layers until ingredients
are used, finishing with a layer of sauce
mixture. Sprinkle cheese on top. Bake at
350°F for 30 minutes, or until golden.

Serves 4.

fettuccine with salmon and asparagus sauce

8 ounces fettuccine

1 (7.5-ounce) can salmon

**1 (12- to 15-ounce) can asparagus
  spears**

¼ cup mayonnaise

**2 tablespoons chopped pecans,
  toasted**

Cook pasta in boiling salted water for
8 to 10 minutes, or until tender. Drain.
Drain salmon, remove bones and flake
fish. Place undrained asparagus in a
blender or processor and blend or process
until smooth. Place in a saucepan along
with salmon and mayonnaise. Bring to
the boil. Serve over fettuccine. Garnish
with pecans.

Serves 4.

from top clockwise, quick storecupboard
seafood lasagne, fettuccine with salmon
and asparagus sauce, macaroni, salmon
and asparagus bake

italian pasta pie

Use any savory pastry for this pie.

1 medium eggplant

Salt

3 cups cooked pasta

2 cups milk

¼ cup all-purpose flour

¼ cup (½ stick) butter or margarine, softened

3 eggs

Salt

Freshly ground black pepper

2 cups grated sharp cheddar cheese

3 zucchini

2 tomatoes

Fresh basil leaves

2 sheets flaky puff pastry

Cut eggplant into slices. Sprinkle both sides with salt. Let stand for a few minutes while preparing rest of ingredients. Drain pasta well. Bring milk to the boil in a large saucepan. Mix flour and butter or margarine together. Remove milk from heat and stir in butter mixture. Cook, stirring, until thick and boiling. Let cool. Lightly beat eggs. Stir pasta, salt, pepper, grated cheese and eggs into milk mixture. Trim zucchini and slice thin. Slice tomatoes. Cut a piece of pastry to fit the bottom of a deep 8-inch cake pan. Prick pastry. Bake at 400°F for 10 minutes. Spread half of the cooled pasta mixture on top of pastry. Rinse eggplant slices and pat dry. Arrange zucchini, eggplant, tomato and basil over pasta. Spread remaining pasta mixture over vegetables. Top with second pastry sheet. Trim to fit. Bake at 400°F for 10 to 15 minutes, then reduce oven temperature to 350°F for 30 minutes, or until golden and cooked. To serve, cut into wedges.

Serves 6.

italian pasta pie

78

seafood and spinach
lasagne

12 ounces skinned and boned fish
  fillets

1 onion

2 cloves garlic

$\frac{1}{2}$ teaspoon grated lemon peel

1 tablespoon lemon juice

Freshly ground black pepper

14 ounces fresh egg lasagne

1 cup grated gruyere cheese

SPINACH SAUCE

1 pound fresh spinach

2 tablespoons butter or margarine

$\frac{1}{4}$ cup all-purpose flour

$1\frac{1}{2}$ cups milk

Salt

Pinch ground nutmeg

Cut fish into strips. Peel and finely chop
onion. Crush and peel garlic. Chop fine.
Mix fish, onion, garlic, lemon peel, lemon
juice and pepper together. Oil a lasagne
dish or baking dish. Cut a sheet of
lasagne to fit the bottom of the dish.
Spread one-half of the fish mixture over
lasagne. Place another sheet of lasagne
on fish and top with half of the spinach
sauce. Repeat layers finishing with a layer
of spinach sauce. Sprinkle with cheese.
Bake at 350°F for 40 minutes, or until fish
is cooked and cheese is golden.

SPINACH SAUCE

Wash spinach and cook in water that
clings to leaves for 4 minutes. Drain.
Squeeze out as much moisture as
possible. Chop spinach fine. Melt butter
or margarine. Stir in flour and cook until
frothy. Remove from heat and stir in
milk. Return to heat and stir until sauce
boils and thickens. Season with salt. Stir
in spinach and nutmeg.

Serves 4 to 6.

seafood and spinach lasagne

roasted bell pepper and eggplant lasagne

Preparing the vegetables for this lasagne is a little fiddly, but the flavor is divine – well worth the effort.

1 medium eggplant

Salt

6 bell peppers, preferably a mixture of red, yellow and green

Vegetable oil

3 zucchini

1 clove garlic

14 ounces fresh spinach lasagne

1 cup grated or shaved parmesan cheese

TOMATO SAUCE

1 onion

2 cloves garlic

2 tablespoons vegetable oil

1 (14- to 16-ounce) can tomatoes in juice

1 teaspoon dried basil

Cut eggplant into $1/2$-inch-thick slices. Sprinkle with salt and let stand while preparing bell peppers. Cut bell peppers in half lengthwise. Remove seeds and stem. Place peppers cut-side down on a baking sheet. Broil for 5 to 10 minutes, or until skins are blistered and brown. Wrap in foil. Wash salt from eggplant and pat dry. Brush eggplant with oil and broil both sides until golden. Cut zucchini in half lengthwise. Crush and peel garlic and rub cut side of zucchini with garlic. Brush zucchini with oil and broil until lightly browned. Peel skins from bell peppers. Cut lasagne to fit a lasagne dish or baking dish. Oil the dish and place a layer of lasagne in bottom of dish. Place a layer of vegetables over lasagne. Top with another layer of lasagne, then a layer of tomato sauce. Repeat layers until all ingredients are used. Top with parmesan cheese. Bake at 350°F for 15 minutes.

TOMATO SAUCE

Peel and chop onion. Crush, peel and chop garlic. Heat oil in a saucepan. Add onion and garlic and cook until clear. Chop tomatoes, removing core. Add tomatoes with their juice to saucepan along with basil. Cook for 5 minutes.

Serves 4.

smoked chicken and spinach lasagne

2 smoked chicken breast halves, skinned and boned

1 pound fresh spinach

14 ounces fresh spinach lasagne

Shaved parmesan cheese

TOMATO SAUCE

1 onion

2 cloves garlic

1 tablespoon vegetable oil

1 teaspoon chili powder

1 (14- to 16-ounce) can tomatoes in juice

1 (15-ounce) can tomato sauce

Cut chicken into thick slices. Wash spinach and cook for 5 minutes in just the water that clings to the leaves. Strain well, squeezing out as much water as possible. Lightly oil a lasagne dish or baking dish. Cut a sheet of lasagne to fit the dish. Place lasagne in the bottom of the dish. Top with one-third of the spinach and chicken. Place another sheet of lasagne on top. Spread one-third of the tomato sauce over the lasagne. Repeat layers, finishing with a layer of tomato sauce. Bake at 350°F for 30 minutes. Sprinkle with parmesan cheese.

TOMATO SAUCE

Peel onion and chop fine. Crush, peel and chop garlic. Heat oil in a saucepan. Add onion and garlic and cook until onion is clear. Stir in chili powder and cook until it smells fragrant. Chop tomatoes. Add tomatoes with their juice and tomato sauce to onion mixture. Cook for 5 minutes.

Serves 4.

roasted bell pepper and eggplant lasagne (top) and smoked chicken and spinach lasagne

lasagne firenze

A cold, wet, spring Sunday in Florence was brightened by this lasagne. It was unlike anything I had tasted before and is a great way to make a little ground beef go a long way.

2 onions

1 bay leaf

6 black peppercorns

2 cups milk

12 ounces lean ground beef

1 (15-ounce) can tomato sauce

¼ cup water

1 teaspoon dried basil

1 teaspoon dried oregano

Salt

Black pepper

¼ cup (½ stick) butter or
   margarine

5 tablespoons all-purpose
   flour

14 ounces fresh lasagne

¼ cup grated or shaved
   parmesan cheese

1 tablespoon chopped fresh
   parsley

Peel and quarter one onion. Place onion, bay leaf, peppercorns and milk in a saucepan. Bring to the boil. Remove from heat and let stand while preparing meat. Brown ground beef in a saucepan. Peel and finely chop second onion. Add to meat and cook for 5 minutes. Add tomato sauce, water, basil and oregano. Cook, uncovered, for 10 minutes. Season with salt and pepper. Melt butter or margarine in a saucepan. Add flour and cook until frothy. Remove from heat and strain in flavored milk. Return to heat and whisk until white sauce boils and thickens. Oil a lasagne dish or other suitable straight-sided baking dish. Cut lasagne to fit dish. Place a layer of lasagne on bottom of dish. Spread a thin layer of white sauce on top. Repeat until all lasagne and white sauce are used, finishing with a layer of lasagne. There will be about six layers. Top with meat sauce. Bake at 375°F for 15 minutes. Sprinkle with parmesan cheese and parsley. Serve with a crisp green salad.

Serves 4 to 6.

lasagne firenze

summer vegetable and
pasta bake

Eggplant is a magnificent vegetable but if it isn't your thing, try using zucchini in this recipe instead. Any cheese of your choice can be used instead of mozzarella.

1 large eggplant
Salt
1 onion
2 cloves garlic
¼ cup vegetable oil, divided
1 (14- to16-ounce) can tomatoes in juice
¼ cup tomato paste
1 teaspoon dried basil
1 teaspoon dried marjoram
Freshly ground black pepper
12 ounces fresh conchiglie
2 cups grated mozzarella cheese

Trim eggplant and cut into slices about ¼-inch thick. Place in a large sieve or colander and sprinkle with salt, making sure cut surfaces of eggplant are lightly covered with salt. Let stand while preparing rest of dish. Peel onion and chop fine. Crush, peel and chop garlic. Heat one tablespoon of oil in a saucepan. Add onion and garlic and cook over low heat for 5 minutes, or until onion is clear. Add tomatoes with their juice, tomato paste, basil, marjoram and pepper and cook for 5 minutes. Wash salt from eggplant and dry with paper towels. Heat remaining oil and quickly fry eggplant slices until golden. Oil a baking dish. Layer one-third of eggplant, pasta, tomato sauce and cheese. Repeat layers twice more. Bake at 350°F for 30 minutes, or until cheese is golden.

Serves 4.

summer vegetable and pasta bake

ham and **egg bake**

Soft bread crumbs are made from stale bread. Make them in a food processor or blender and store in the freezer until required.

1/4 cup (1/2 stick) butter or margarine

1/4 cup all-purpose flour

3 cups low-fat milk

Salt

Freshly ground black pepper

2 teaspoons Dijon mustard

14 ounces fresh spinach fettuccine

4 hard-cooked eggs

1 ham steak

1 cup grated sharp cheddar cheese

1/2 cup soft bread crumbs

Melt butter or margarine in a saucepan. Stir in flour and cook until frothy. Remove from heat and slowly stir in milk, salt, pepper and mustard. Return to heat and cook, stirring, until sauce boils and thickens. Cut fettuccine in half and add to sauce. Peel eggs, then coarsely chop. Cut rind and fat from ham steak. Cut meat into 1/2-inch cubes. Stir eggs and ham into sauce. Pour mixture into a baking dish. Sprinkle with cheese and bread crumbs. Bake at 350°F for 20 minutes, or until golden.

Serves 4.

zucchini and tomato **pasta bake**

14 ounces spaghetti

6 medium zucchini

1 (14- to 16-ounce) can Italian-style tomatoes

1 (15-ounce) can tomato sauce

1 teaspoon chili powder

1 cup grated sharp cheddar cheese

Cook spaghetti in boiling salted water for 8 to 10 minutes, or until tender. Drain well. Wash and trim zucchini. Cut in half lengthwise. Place spaghetti in bottom of an oiled shallow baking dish. Arrange zucchini cut-side down over spaghetti. Mix tomatoes with their juice, tomato sauce and chili powder together. Pour tomato mixture over zucchini. Sprinkle with cheese. Bake at 350°F for 30 minutes, or until bubbling.

Serves 4 to 6.

ham and egg bake (top) and zucchini and tomato pasta bake

quick **cannelloni**

FILLING

1 pound lean ground beef

1 onion

2 cloves garlic

1 teaspoon dried basil

1 teaspoon dried marjoram

¼ cup tomato paste

2 eggs

½ cup milk

14 ounces fresh lasagne

1 (14- to 16-ounce) jar pasta sauce

1 cup grated sharp cheddar cheese

FILLING

Brown beef in a skillet. Peel and chop onion. Crush, peel and chop garlic. Add onion and garlic to pan and cook for 5 minutes, or until onion is clear. Add basil, marjoram and tomato paste. Mix well. Remove from heat. Beat eggs and milk together and stir into meat mixture.

Cut lasagne into 4-inch pieces. Place about three tablespoons of filling down center of each piece of pasta. Roll pasta around filling and place, cut-side down, in an oiled baking dish. Pour pasta sauce over rolls. Sprinkle with grated cheese. Bake at 350ºF for 20 minutes, or until pasta is tender and cheese is golden.

Serves 4 to 6.

quick cannelloni

pasta and **lentil brew**

1 cup brown lentils
4 cups chicken stock
1 (14- to 16-ounce) can Mexican-style
tomatoes
8 ounces fresh or frozen cheese and
spinach ravioli
3 tablespoons finely chopped fresh
parsley

Wash lentils. Place lentils and chicken
stock in a large saucepan. Bring to the
boil and simmer for 25 minutes, or until
tender. Puree lentils and cooking liquid in
a food processor or blender. Return to
saucepan. Add tomatoes with their juice
and ravioli. Bring to the boil and cook for
10 minutes, or until ravioli is tender.
Garnish with parsley.

Serves 4.

cottage cheese
and pesto lasagne

14 ounces fresh lasagne
½ cup pesto
1 (16-ounce) carton cottage cheese
1 (14- to 16-ounce) can Italian-style
tomatoes
1 cup grated sharp cheddar cheese

Place a layer of lasagne in bottom of
greased dish. Top with pesto and cottage
cheese. Repeat layers until ingredients
are used. Pour tomatoes and juice
over layers. Sprinkle with
cheese. Bake at 375°F for
15 to 20 minutes, or
until lasagne is tender.

Serves 4.

pasta and lentil brew (top) and
cottage cheese and pesto lasagne

robanesca pasta sauce

There's a traditional pasta sauce called Puttanesca with olives, tomatoes and anchovies as the basic ingredients. I'm not a great fan of anchovies, so I have taken this idea and combined it with some other flavors, hence the name.

14 ounces fettuccine

2 tablespoons chopped fresh parsley

ROBANESCA SAUCE

3 cloves garlic

1 tablespoon vegetable oil

1 (14- to 16-ounce) can chunky tomato and onion

1 teaspoon dried oregano

¼ cup red wine vinegar

1 cup pitted prunes

½ cup pimiento-stuffed green olives

½ cup capers

2 bay leaves

¼ cup dry white wine

¼ teaspoon chili powder

1 tablespoon brown sugar

Cook pasta in boiling salted water for 8 to 10 minutes, or until tender. Drain well. Toss pasta with Robanesca Sauce and garnish with parsley.

ROBANESCA SAUCE

Crush, peel and chop garlic. Heat oil in a saucepan. Add garlic and cook and stir for 1 to 2 minutes, or until it starts to turn golden. Add tomato and onion with juice, oregano, vinegar, prunes, olives, capers, bay leaves, wine, chili powder and brown sugar. Boil, uncovered, for 10 minutes, stirring occasionally.

Serves 4.

pasta
with tomato sauce

I use this tomato sauce with just about anything. It's great with crumbed schnitzel or other meats, as well as any pasta dish.

1 pound beef ravioli

Fresh basil leaves or parsley

TOMATO SAUCE

1 onion

2 cloves garlic

2 tablespoons vegetable oil

1 (14- to 16-ounce) can tomatoes in juice

1 teaspoon dried basil

2 tablespoons tomato paste

Freshly ground black pepper

Cook pasta in boiling salted water for 8 to 10 minutes, or until tender. Drain well. Pour Tomato Sauce over pasta. Garnish with basil or parsley.

TOMATO SAUCE

Peel onion and chop fine. Crush, peel and chop garlic. Heat oil in a saucepan. Add onion and garlic and cook for 5 minutes, or until onion is clear. Add tomatoes with juice, breaking up tomatoes with a wooden spoon. Add basil, tomato paste and pepper. Cook for 10 minutes, stirring occasionally.

Serves 4.

pasta with roasted bell pepper sauce

Roasting or broiling peppers fills the house with the most delicious smell. It is a little fiddly removing the skins, but it's cheaper than buying ready-done products.

8 ounces chicken agnolotti or cheese and spinach tortellini

Chopped green onions (green part only)

ROASTED BELL PEPPER SAUCE

3 red bell peppers

2 onions

4 cloves garlic

1 tablespoon vegetable oil

1 teaspoon chili powder

½ cup tomato sauce

Freshly ground black pepper

Cook pasta in boiling salted water for 8 to 10 minutes, or until tender. Drain well. Pour Roasted Bell Pepper Sauce over pasta. Garnish with green onions.

ROASTED BELL PEPPER SAUCE

Cut bell peppers in half vertically. Remove seeds and cores. Place cut-side down on a baking sheet and broil until skins blister. Remove from oven and let stand until cool enough to handle. Peel off skins. Peel onions and chop fine. Crush, peel and chop garlic. Heat oil in a skillet. Add onion and garlic and cook for 5 minutes, or until onion is clear. Add chili powder and cook for 30 seconds. Place bell peppers, onion mixture, tomato sauce and pepper in the bowl of a food processor or blender and puree.

Serves 4.

from back clockwise: robanesca pasta sauce, pasta with roasted bell pepper sauce and pasta with tomato sauce

pasta with
fresh tomato sauce

*If you have some wine on hand you can spare
for cooking, try this for a full-flavored tomato
sauce.*

1 pound cheese and spinach tortellini
Fresh herbs

TOMATO SAUCE
1 clove garlic
1 tablespoon vegetable oil
1 cup frozen stir-fry vegetables,
   thawed
1 (15-ounce) can tomato sauce
1/2 cup dry red wine
1 teaspoon dried thyme
1 teaspoon dried marjoram
Freshly ground black pepper
1 teaspoon granulated sugar

Cook pasta in boiling salted water for
8 to 10 minutes, or until tender. Drain
well. Reheat sauce if necessary. Pour
Tomato Sauce over pasta and garnish
with fresh herbs. Serve immediately.

TOMATO SAUCE

Crush and peel garlic. Heat oil in a
saucepan. Add garlic and vegetables
and cook for 5 minutes. Add tomato
sauce, wine, thyme, marjoram, pepper
and sugar. Cook for 10 minutes, stirring
occasionally. Puree mixture in a food
processor or blender.

Serves 4.

**from back left clockwise: pasta with
fresh tomato sauce, pasta with
lemon and herb sauce and
tuscan peas with pasta**

tuscan peas
with pasta

14 ounces tri-color fettuccine
Freshly ground black pepper
Fresh herbs
TUSCAN PEAS
1 onion
2 cloves garlic
2 slices bacon
2 tablespoons vegetable oil
1 cup chicken stock
1½ teaspoons dried sage
3 cups frozen peas
1 teaspoon salt

Cook pasta in boiling salted water for 8 to 10 minutes, or until tender. Drain well. Toss pasta with pea mixture. Grind pepper over all. Serve garnished with fresh herbs.

TUSCAN PEAS

Peel onion and chop fine. Crush, peel and chop garlic. Finely chop bacon. Heat oil in a saucepan. Add onion, garlic and bacon and cook for 5 minutes, or until onion is clear. Add chicken stock and sage and bring to the boil. Add peas. Cover and cook for 10 minutes. Season with salt. Do not drain peas before adding to pasta.

Serves 4.

pasta with lemon
and herb sauce

1 pound veal tortellini
Fresh herbs
LEMON AND HERB SAUCE
1 (8-ounce) carton low-fat sour cream
¼ cup lemon juice
½ cup chopped fresh chives
½ cup chopped fresh parsley
1 teaspoon grated lemon peel
Pinch ground red (cayenne) pepper
Pinch ground nutmeg

Cook pasta in boiling salted water for 8 to 10 minutes, or until tender. Drain well. Toss pasta with Lemon and Herb Sauce and garnish with fresh herbs.

LEMON AND HERB SAUCE

Mix sour cream, lemon juice, chives, parsley, lemon peel, red pepper and nutmeg together in a saucepan. Bring to boiling point, but do not boil.

Serves 4.

new world
bolognese sauce

1 onion
1 tablespoon vegetable oil
1 pound lean ground beef
1 (14-16-ounce) can Italian-style
    tomatoes
$^1/_4$ cup tomato paste
1 teaspoon dried oregano
$^1/_2$ teaspoon dried thyme
$^1/_2$ cup beef stock
Salt
Black pepper
14 ounces fettuccine

Peel onion and chop fine. Heat oil in a
saucepan. Add onion and cook for
5 minutes, or until onion is clear. Add
meat and cook until lightly browned,
breaking it up with a wooden spoon.
Add tomatoes with their juice, tomato
paste, oregano, thyme, beef stock, salt
and pepper to meat. Bring to the boil,
then reduce heat and simmer, uncovered,
for 30 minutes, or until sauce is thick.
Cook fettuccine in boiling salted water
for 5 minutes, or until tender. Drain.
Serve sauce over cooked pasta.

Serves 4 to 6.

blt pasta with
chili mayonnaise

14 ounces tri-color fettuccine
8 slices bacon
4 eggs
4 lettuce leaves
2 tomatoes
$^1/_4$ teaspoon chili powder
$^1/_2$ cup mayonnaise

Cook pasta in boiling salted water for
8 to 10 minutes, or until tender. Drain.
Cut bacon into thin strips and cook in a
skillet until crisp. Drain on absorbent
paper. Remove any fat from pan, then fry
eggs in pan. Wash, dry and shred lettuce.
Remove core and dice tomatoes. Mix chili
powder into mayonnaise. Arrange bacon,
eggs, lettuce and tomatoes over cooked
pasta. Top with chili mayonnaise. Serve
immediately.

Serves 4.

92

bolognese sauce

There are many versions of this famous sauce and this does not purport to be authentic, for a true bolognese sauce takes many hours to prepare. This recipe is more along the lines of a traditional sauce.

1 onion
2 ribs celery
2 carrots
3 slices bacon
1 tablespoon vegetable oil
1 pound lean ground beef
Salt
Freshly ground black pepper
Pinch ground nutmeg
$\frac{1}{2}$ cup dry white wine
1 cup water
2 beef bouillon cubes, crumbled
1 (15-ounce) can tomato sauce
14 ounces spaghetti

Peel onion and chop fine. Wash, trim and slice celery. Peel and chop carrots. Chop bacon. Heat oil in a large saucepan. Add onion, celery, carrot and bacon and cook for 5 minutes. Add ground beef and cook until it changes color. Season with salt, pepper and nutmeg. Stir in wine and water. Add bouillon cubes. Cook, uncovered, until most of liquid has evaporated. Add tomato sauce. Cook for 5 minutes. Cook pasta in boiling salted water for 8 to 10 minutes, or until tender. Serve Bolognese Sauce over cooked pasta.

Serves 4 to 6.

from back left clockwise: bolognese sauce, new world bolognese sauce and blt pasta with chili mayonnaise

creamy **seafood** sauce

Use a mix of fresh fish fillets, scallops, prawns, crab sticks, mussels, smoked salmon or whatever your budget and taste runs to.

14 ounces tagliatelle
1 pound fresh mixed fish
1 cup chicken stock
1 onion
2 tablespoons butter or margarine
3 tablespoons all-purpose flour
1 (8-ounce) carton low-fat sour cream
2 tablespoons chopped fresh parsley

Cook pasta in boiling salted water for 8 to 10 minutes, or until tender. Drain. Prepare fish as necessary. Cut fillets into $3/4$-inch cubes. Heat chicken stock in a skillet and poach fish until cooked. Drain, reserving stock. Peel onion and chop fine. Melt butter or margarine in a saucepan. Add onion and cook for 5 minutes, or until clear. Stir in flour and cook until frothy. Pour in reserved stock and cook, stirring, until sauce boils and thickens. Stir in sour cream, parsley and fish. Bring to boil, but do not boil. Serve over cooked pasta.

Serves 4.

pasta **frittata**

This is a great way to use leftover pasta. Any variety will do.

3 slices bacon
2 to 3 cups cooked pasta
6 eggs
Salt
Freshly ground black pepper
$1/4$ cup chopped fresh parsley

Place bacon in bottom of a large oiled skillet. Top with pasta, spreading to cover pan. Lightly beat eggs. Season with salt and pepper. Stir in parsley. Pour egg mixture over pasta. Cook over medium heat until frittata is browned and set and bacon is cooked. Turn and cook other side. Serve with a green salad.

Serves 4 to 6.

from back left clockwise: carbonara, creamy seafood sauce and pasta frittata

carbonara

5 slices bacon
2 cloves garlic
$\frac{1}{2}$ cup low-fat half-and-half or light
cream
14 ounces fettuccine
2 eggs
Salt
Freshly ground black pepper
$\frac{1}{4}$ cup grated parmesan cheese
Additional parmesan cheese, for
garnish

Cut bacon into thin strips. Crush, peel
and chop garlic. Cook bacon in a skillet
until crisp. Add garlic and cook for
1 minute. Pour in cream and mix well.
Cook pasta in boiling salted water for
8 to 10 minutes, or until tender. Drain
well. Beat eggs, salt, pepper and $\frac{1}{4}$ cup
parmesan cheese together. Add drained
pasta to bacon mixture in skillet. Mix
well. Add egg mixture and toss until
combined. Cook over low heat if
necessary to set eggs. Serve immediately,
garnished with parmesan cheese.

Serves 4.

spaghetti with **meatballs**

1 onion
1 pound lean ground beef
2 tablespoons ketchup
2 teaspoons Worcestershire sauce
1 egg
$\frac{1}{2}$ cup soft bread crumbs
1 beef bouillon cube, crumbled
1 tablespoon vegetable oil
1 (14- to 16-ounce) can Italian-style
  tomatoes
1 (15-ounce) can tomato sauce
14 ounces spaghetti

Peel onion and chop fine. Mix onion, ground beef, ketchup, Worcestershire sauce, egg, bread crumbs and bouillon cube together until well combined. Take tablespoonsful of mixture and form into balls. Heat oil in a large skillet and cook meatballs for 10 minutes, or until cooked. Add tomatoes with their juice and tomato sauce and bring to the boil. Cook pasta in boiling salted water for 8 to 10 minutes, or until tender. Drain. Serve meatballs over spaghetti.

Serves 4 to 6.

sausage ball sauce

1 pound bulk pork sausage
$\frac{1}{2}$ cup dried bread crumbs
2 tablespoons vegetable oil
$\frac{1}{4}$ teaspoon chili powder
1 teaspoon ground coriander
1 (14- to 16-ounce) can Italian-style
  tomatoes
1 green bell pepper
14 ounces tri-color fettuccine

Divide sausage into 16 portions. Roll in crumbs and form into ball shapes. Heat oil in a skillet and cook sausage balls for about 10 minutes, or until cooked. Drain. While sausage balls are cooking, mix chili, coriander and tomatoes with their juice in a saucepan. Seed bell pepper and cut into strips. Add bell pepper to tomato mixture and heat until boiling. Add sausage balls to tomato mixture. Cook pasta in boiling salted water for 8 to 10 minutes, or until tender. Drain. Serve tomato mixture over pasta.

Serves 4.

**spaghetti with meatballs (top)
and sausage ball sauce**

mexican pasta sauce

1 pound lean ground beef
1 teaspoon ground cumin
2 (14- to 16-ounce) cans Mexican-
    style tomatoes
1/2 teaspoon dried oregano
1 teaspoon salt
14 ounces tagliatelle
3 tomatoes
1 red onion
2 tablespoons chopped fresh parsley
1 avocado

Brown ground beef in a saucepan. Add cumin and cook for 1 minute, or until cumin smells fragrant. Add canned tomatoes with their juice, oregano and salt. Cook, uncovered, for 10 minutes. Cook pasta until tender. Drain. Remove cores from fresh tomatoes and chop into 1/4-inch cubes. Peel onion and chop fine. Mix tomatoes, onion and parsley together to make a salsa. Peel, pit and slice avocado. Serve meat sauce over cooked pasta. Top with tomato salsa and avocado. Serve immediately.

Serves 4.

mushroom
and meat sauce

14 ounces fettuccine
4 slices veal or chicken schnitzel
2 cloves garlic
4 ounces fresh button mushrooms
2 tablespoons vegetable oil
2 tablespoons dry sherry
2 tablespoons tomato paste
1 (8-ounce) carton low-fat sour cream
Freshly ground black pepper
2 tablespoons chopped fresh parsley

Cook fettuccine in boiling salted water for 8 to 10 minutes, or until tender. Drain. Cut schnitzels into 1/2-inch strips. Crush, peel and chop garlic. Wipe, trim and slice mushrooms. Heat oil in a skillet. Add schnitzel strips and garlic and cook until meat is just cooked. Add mushrooms and cook for 2 minutes. Add sherry, tomato paste and sour cream. Mix well and bring to the boil, but do not boil. Season with pepper. Serve with cooked fettuccine and garnish with parsley.

Serves 4.

mushroom and meat sauce
(top) and mexican pasta sauce

curried chicken sauce

14 ounces tagliatelle

1 onion

2 cloves garlic

2 tablespoons vegetable oil

16 to18 ounces chicken tenderloins

1 tablespoon curry powder

$\frac{1}{2}$ cup coconut milk

1 cup plain yogurt

2 tablespoons chopped fresh
coriander or parsley

Cook pasta in boiling salted water for 8 to 10 minutes, or until tender. Drain. Peel onion and chop fine. Crush, peel and chop garlic. Heat oil in a skillet. Add chicken and quickly cook until barely done. Add onion and garlic and cook and stir for 2 minutes. Add curry powder and cook for 1 minute, or until curry smells fragrant. Add coconut milk, yogurt and coriander or parsley. Bring to boiling point, but do not boil. Serve sauce over cooked pasta.

Serves 4.

chicken and tarragon sauce

14 ounces spaghetti

1 onion

2 cloves garlic

4 ounces fresh button mushrooms

1 tablespoon vegetable oil

2 cups diced cooked chicken

2 teaspoons dried tarragon

2 cups plain yogurt

2 tablespoons mayonnaise

1 tablespoon chopped fresh parsley

Cook pasta in boiling salted water for 8 to 10 minutes, or until tender. Drain. Peel onion and chop fine. Crush, peel and chop garlic. Wipe and trim mushrooms. Slice mushrooms if large. Heat oil in a saucepan. Add onion and garlic and cook and stir for 5 minutes, or until onion is clear. Add mushrooms and chicken and cook and stir for 3 minutes. Add tarragon, yogurt and mayonnaise. Bring to boiling point, but do not boil. Serve sauce over cooked pasta. Garnish with chopped parsley.

Serves 4.

curried chicken sauce and
chicken tarragon sauce

quick **fettuccine** with chickpeas

14 ounces spinach fettuccine

1 onion

2 cloves garlic

2 tablespoons vegetable oil

2 (15-ounce) cans chickpeas or
    garbanzo beans

1 teaspoon dried sage

1 teaspoon dried basil

Freshly ground black pepper

Shaved parmesan cheese

Cook pasta in boiling salted water for
8 to 10 minutes, or until tender. Drain.
Peel onion and chop fine. Crush, peel
and chop garlic. Heat oil in a skillet. Add
onion and garlic and cook for 5 minutes,
or until onion is clear. Drain chickpeas.
Add to skillet, then stir in hot pasta, sage
and basil. Heat over low heat for 2 to 3
minutes. Season with pepper. Serve
immediately, garnished with parmesan
cheese.

Serves 4.

egg and tomato **pasta**

12 ounces tri-color fettuccine

6 eggs

1 (14- to 16-ounce) can chunky
    tomato and onion

2 tablespoons chopped fresh parsley

BUTTERED CRUMBS

2 cloves garlic

¼ cup (½ stick) butter or margarine

½ cup soft bread crumbs

Cook pasta in boiling salted water for
8 to 10 minutes, or until tender. Drain.
Hard-cook eggs. Peel, then cut into
quarters. Heat tomato and onion with
juice in a saucepan. Stir in parsley. Pour
over pasta. Arrange eggs on top of
tomato mixture. Sprinkle buttered
crumbs over all.

BUTTERED CRUMBS

Crush, peel and chop garlic. Melt
butter or margarine in a skillet. Add
garlic and cook and stir for 2 minutes.
Add bread crumbs and cook until just
golden.

Serves 4 to 6.

**quick fettuccine with chickpeas (top)
and egg and tomato pasta**

pasta with garlic and parsley sauce

14 ounces fettuccine

Freshly ground black pepper

GARLIC AND PARSLEY SAUCE

4 cloves garlic

$\frac{1}{4}$ cup vegetable oil

$\frac{1}{4}$ cup chopped fresh parsley

Cook pasta in boiling salted water for 8 to 10 minutes, or until tender. Drain well. Toss pasta with Garlic and Parsley Sauce. Season with pepper and serve immediately.

GARLIC AND PARSLEY SAUCE

Crush and peel garlic and chop fine. Heat oil in a skillet. Add garlic and cook gently over low heat for 2 to 3 minutes. Remove from heat. Stir in parsley.

Serves 4.

pasta with mushroom sauce

14 ounces fettuccine

2 tablespoons chopped fresh parsley

MUSHROOM SAUCE

12 ounces button mushrooms

1 onion

2 cloves garlic

2 tablespoons vegetable oil

1 (1$\frac{1}{4}$-ounce) envelope dry mushroom soup mix

1 cup milk

2 tablespoons dry sherry

Cook pasta in boiling salted water for 8 to 10 minutes, or until tender. Drain well. Pour Mushroom Sauce over pasta. Garnish with parsley. Serve immediately.

MUSHROOM SAUCE

Wipe mushrooms and trim. Cut mushrooms in half. Peel onion and chop fine. Crush, peel and chop garlic. Heat oil in a saucepan. Add onion, garlic and mushrooms and cook for 5 minutes. Mix soup mix with milk and sherry and add to saucepan. Cook, stirring, until mixture comes to the boil. Simmer for 5 minutes.

Serves 4.

pasta with garlic and parsley sauce (top) and pasta with mushroom sauce

sweet treats

Do sweet things for other people, then do them for yourself. It's OK to indulge – and it's fun to play with ingredients that hold so much promise of pleasure. Three cheers for sugary, gooey, sticky, rich and creamy!

almond macaroons

2 egg whites
$\frac{1}{2}$ cup superfine granulated sugar
5 ounces ground almonds
$\frac{1}{4}$ teaspoon almond extract
3 tablespoons confectioners' sugar,
   divided

Beat egg whites until soft peaks form.
Add superfine sugar a little at a time.
Continue beating until meringue is thick
and glossy. Fold ground almonds, almond
extract and two tablespoons of
confectioners' sugar into meringue. Fill a
piping bag fitted with a large plain
nozzle and pipe 1$\frac{1}{2}$-inch oval lengths
onto a baking sheet lined with parchment
or waxed paper. Dust with remaining
tablespoon of confectioners' sugar. Bake
at 325°F for 25 minutes, or until lightly
browned. Let cool on baking sheet. Store
in an airtight container. Serve with ice
cream or coffee.

Makes about 20.

florentines

7 tablespoons (1 stick minus
   1 tablespoon) butter
$\frac{1}{2}$ cup superfine granulated sugar
1 tablespoon milk
3 tablespoons all-purpose flour
$\frac{1}{4}$ cup finely chopped mixed candied
   peel
$\frac{1}{2}$ cup coarsely chopped flaked
   almonds
$\frac{1}{4}$ cup mixed dried fruit
3$\frac{1}{2}$ ounces baking chocolate

Put butter, sugar and milk in a saucepan.
Melt over low heat, stirring constantly,
until sugar dissolves. Bring to the boil and
cook for 1 minute. Remove from heat.
Add flour, mixed peel, almonds and mixed
fruit. Place teaspoons of mixture onto a
baking sheet lined with parchment or
waxed paper, leaving plenty of room for
spreading. Flatten slightly. Bake at 350°F
for 7 to 10 minutes, or until golden. Let
cool slightly and reshape if necessary.
Transfer to a cooling rack to cool
completely. Melt chocolate over hot
water. Spread chocolate over flat side of
florentines. Make a wavy pattern in
chocolate and let set. Store in an airtight
container.

Makes about 15.

florentines and almond macaroons

fig and toasted almond cake

Toast almonds at 350°F for 7 to 10 minutes. Toasted nuts have much better flavor and texture in any dish.

1 cup chopped dried figs
$\frac{1}{2}$ cup boiling water
1 cup whole blanched almonds, toasted
4 egg whites
$\frac{1}{2}$ cup packed brown sugar
1 tablespoon confectioners' sugar
$\frac{1}{2}$ teaspoon ground cinnamon
SPICED CREAM
1 cup heavy or whipping cream
1 teaspoon ground cinnamon

Cook figs in boiling water for 10 minutes. Let cool. Stir in almonds. Beat egg whites and brown sugar together until stiff peaks form. Fold fig-almond mixture into meringue. Spread mixture in an 8-inch round loose-bottom cake pan lined with parchment or waxed paper. Bake at 350°F for 45 minutes, or until lightly golden and set. Let cool for 10 minutes before removing from pan. When ready to serve, mix confectioners' sugar and cinnamon together. Sprinkle over cake. Serve with Spiced Cream.

SPICED CREAM

Beat cream and cinnamon until soft peaks form.

Serves 6 to 8.

italian fig cake

2 eggs
$\frac{3}{4}$ cup granulated sugar
1 cup all-purpose flour
1$\frac{1}{2}$ teaspoons baking powder
$\frac{1}{4}$ cup milk
1 tablespoon toasted bread crumbs
Confectioners' sugar
FILLING
1$\frac{1}{2}$ cups chopped dried figs
$\frac{3}{4}$ cup finely chopped walnuts
$\frac{1}{2}$ cup orange marmalade
2 teaspoons grated orange peel
$\frac{1}{8}$ teaspoon ground cloves
$\frac{1}{2}$ teaspoon ground cinnamon

Beat eggs and sugar together until light and thick. Sift together flour and baking powder. Fold flour mixture alternately with milk into egg mixture. Grease sides of an 8-inch cake pan and line bottom with parchment or waxed paper. Sprinkle bread crumbs in pan. Spoon half the cake batter into cake pan. Carefully dot fig filling on batter, then spread it over batter. Spread remaining batter over filling. Bake at 350°F for 35 to 40 minutes, or until an inserted skewer comes out clean. Dust with confectioners' sugar. Serve warm as a dessert cake or cold with tea or coffee.

FILLING

Mix all ingredients together.

Serves 6.

espresso cake

1 cup boiling water

¼ cup ground espresso coffee beans

⅞ cup (1 stick plus 6 tablespoons) butter

1¼ cups granulated sugar

3 eggs

1 tablespoon vanilla extract

2 cups all-purpose flour

3 teaspoons baking powder

¼ cup finely ground espresso coffee beans

8 sugar cubes

Ground cinnamon

COFFEE-FLAVORED CREAM

1 cup heavy or whipping cream

1 tablespoon confectioners' sugar

2 tablespoons very strong espresso coffee

Pour boiling water over ¼ cup ground coffee beans and let steep for 5 minutes. Strain liquid from beans. Pour liquid over butter in a large bowl, stirring until butter melts. Stir in sugar, eggs and vanilla. Beat with a wooden spoon until combined. Sift flour and baking powder into mixture. Add ¼ cup finely ground coffee beans and stir to mix. Pour batter into an 8-inch square cake pan lined with parchment or waxed paper. Bake at 350°F for 50 to 55 minutes, or until cake springs back when lightly touched. Crush sugar cubes. Sprinkle sugar over hot cake. Let cool in pan for 10 minutes before turning onto a cooling rack. Dust with cinnamon and serve with Coffee-Flavored Cream.

COFFEE-FLAVORED CREAM

Whip cream until soft. Beat in confectioners' sugar and coffee.

Serves 8 to 10.

fig and toasted almond cake,
espresso cake and italian fig cake (left)

apricot cake

2 (15-ounce) cans apricot halves in
    natural juice
1/2 cup (1 stick) butter
1 cup granulated sugar
2 eggs
2 cups all-purpose flour
4 teaspoons baking powder
TOPPING
1/4 cup all-purpose flour
1/4 cup rolled oats, uncooked
2 tablespoons brown sugar
1 teaspoon baking powder
1/4 cup (1/2 stick) butter

Puree one can of apricots with their juice
in a food processor or blender. Drain
second can of apricots. Melt butter in a
saucepan large enough to hold all the
ingredients. Stir in sugar. Beat in eggs,
flour, baking powder and apricot puree
with a wooden spoon. Pour batter into
an 8-inch round deep cake pan lined with
parchment or waxed paper. Arrange
drained apricots on surface of batter.
Sprinkle with topping. Bake at 350°F for
1 hour, or until an inserted skewer comes
out clean. Serve warm with whipped
cream if wished.

TOPPING

Mix flour, rolled oats, brown sugar and
baking powder together. Rub in butter
until mixture resembles coarse crumbs.

Serves 8 to 10.

lemon semolina cake

Semolina is usually found in the cereal or
flour section of the supermarket.

1/2 cup (1 stick) butter
1 cup granulated sugar
3 eggs
2 teaspoons grated lemon peel
1/2 cup semolina
1 cup all-purpose flour
2 teaspoons baking powder
1/4 cup lemon juice
1/4 cup confectioners' sugar

Melt butter in a saucepan large
enough to hold all the ingredients.
Remove from heat and stir in sugar.
Add eggs, lemon peel and semolina.
Beat until well combined. Sift flour and
baking powder into mixture and mix
thoroughly. Pour batter into an 8-inch
round cake pan lined with parchment or
waxed paper. Bake at 350°F for 35 minutes.
Mix lemon juice and confectioners' sugar
together. Remove cake from oven and
pour lemon juice mixture over cake.
Return to oven and bake for 10 minutes.
Serve warm or at room
temperature.

Serves 6 to 8.

apricot cake,
and lemon semolina cake

summer **berry pie**

6 cups mixed fresh or frozen berries,
    such as blueberries, raspberries or
    blackberries

2 tablespoons cornstarch

2 tablespoons water

1$\frac{1}{2}$ cups all-purpose flour

$\frac{1}{2}$ cup custard powder (see note)

$\frac{1}{4}$ cup confectioners' sugar

1 (8-ounce) package cream cheese

$\frac{1}{4}$ cup water

Confectioners' sugar

Thaw berries if frozen. Place berries in a
saucepan. Heat gently. Mix cornstarch
and water together and stir into berries.
Cook until mixture boils and thickens. Let
cool. While berry mixture is cooling, place
flour, custard powder and confectioners'
sugar in the bowl of a food processor or
a bowl. Cut in cream cheese until mixture
resembles coarse crumbs. Add enough
water to form a stiff dough. Roll out
dough on a lightly floured surface. Line
an 8-inch flan pan or pie plate with
pastry. Reroll pastry scraps and use to
make decorative shapes. Bake shapes
with pastry shell. Bake pastry shell blind
at 375°F for 15 minutes. Remove baking
blind material and return pastry shell to
oven for 3 minutes to dry out. Let cool,
then fill with berry mixture. Arrange
pastry shapes over berries. Dust with
confectioners' sugar and serve.

Serves 6.

NOTE: Custard powder is available in
specialty food shops or by mail order. You
can substitute an equal amount of instant
vanilla pudding and pie filling mix (dry).

summer berry pie and cappuccino pie

cappuccino pie

BASE

1 (8.5-ounce) package chocolate wafers

¼ cup (½ stick) butter, melted

1 tablespoon instant coffee powder

FILLING

1 cup milk

2 tablespoons instant coffee powder

¼ cup granulated sugar

¼ cup cornstarch

2 egg yolks

TOPPING

2 egg whites

½ cup granulated sugar

½ teaspoon unsweetened cocoa powder

Chocolate sprinkles

Crush chocolate wafers into medium-fine crumbs in a food processor or thick plastic bag. Add melted butter and coffee powder and mix to combine. Press mixture into the bottom of an 8-inch springform pan or loose-bottom cake pan. Refrigerate while preparing filling. Pour filling into base. Spread topping over filling. Bake at 375°F for 10 minutes, or until just starting to color. Dust with cocoa powder and garnish with chocolate sprinkles.

FILLING

Whisk milk, coffee, sugar and cornstarch together. Heat, stirring constantly, until mixture boils and thickens. Remove from heat and stir in egg yolks. Pour into prepared base.

TOPPING

Beat egg whites until stiff. Gradually beat in sugar until mixture is thick and glossy.

Serves 4 to 6.

luscious lemon tart

14 ounces sweet short pastry (your favorite recipe, or use refrigerated pie crusts)

Confectioners' sugar

FILLING

4 eggs

2 egg yolks

$\frac{1}{4}$ cup lemon juice

1 tablespoon finely grated lemon peel

$\frac{1}{4}$ cup granulated sugar

1 (8-ounce) carton sour cream

PASSION LEMON CREAM

$\frac{1}{2}$ cup sour cream

1 teaspoon grated lemon peel

$\frac{1}{4}$ cup passionfruit pulp

Roll out pastry on a lightly floured surface to $\frac{1}{4}$-inch thickness. Use to line an 8-inch loose-bottom flan pan or a 14 x $4\frac{1}{2}$-inch fluted oblong tart pan. Bake blind at 375°F for 10 minutes. Remove baking blind material and return to oven for 2 to 3 minutes to dry out. Let cool while preparing filling. Pour filling into pastry. Bake at 325°F for 35 to 40 minutes, or until filling is set. Let cool. Remove from pan. Serve dusted with confectioners' sugar and accompanied by Passion Lemon Cream.

FILLING

Lightly beat eggs, egg yolks, lemon juice, lemon peel and sugar together until combined. Beat sour cream with a spoon to soften, then stir it into egg mixture until combined. Pour mixture through a sieve into pastry shell.

PASSION LEMON CREAM

Mix sour cream, lemon peel and passionfruit pulp together. Use two warm tablespoons to shape mixture into ovals.

Serves 6 to 8.

lemon cornmeal cake

3 eggs

2 egg whites

1 cup granulated sugar

2 tablespoons grated lemon peel

2 tablespoons lemon juice

$\frac{1}{2}$ cup sour cream

1 cup yellow cornmeal

$\frac{1}{2}$ cup all-purpose flour

2 teaspoons baking powder

Confectioners' sugar

LEMON SOUR CREAM

1 (8-ounce) carton sour cream

1 tablespoon grated lemon peel

1 tablespoon lemon juice

Beat eggs, egg whites and sugar together until light and creamy. Fold in lemon peel, lemon juice, sour cream, cornmeal, flour and baking powder until just combined. Pour batter into an 8-inch round cake pan lined with parchment or waxed paper. Bake at 350°F for 35 minutes, or until cake is just cooked. Serve warm, dusted with confectioners' sugar and accompanied by Lemon Sour Cream.

LEMON SOUR CREAM

Mix sour cream, lemon peel and lemon juice together.

Serves 6 to 8.

luscious lemon tart (bottom) and lemon cornmeal cake

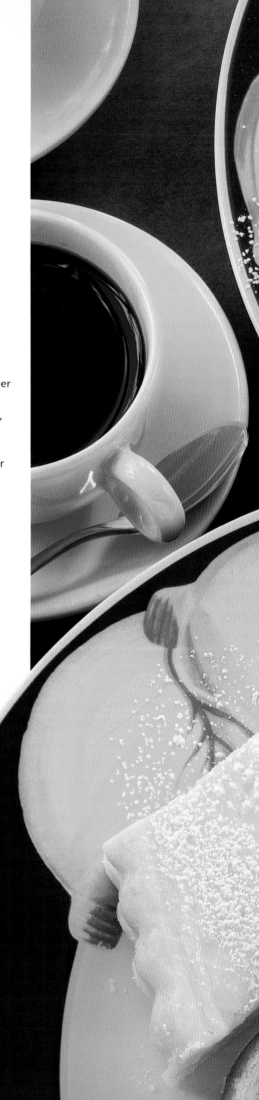

tiramisu

5 tablespoons custard powder (see note)

3 cups milk, divided

3 tablespoons granulated sugar

1 egg white

$1/2$ cup brandy, divided

1 (5- to 6-ounce) package lady fingers

1 (8-ounce) carton cream cheese

$1/4$ cup strong black coffee

1 cup heavy or whipping cream

Mix custard powder with $1/4$ cup of milk. Heat remaining $2^3/4$ cups milk. Pour heated milk onto custard powder mixture. Return to saucepan. Stir in sugar. Cook over medium heat, stirring constantly, until mixture boils and thickens. Remove from heat. Allow to cool. Beat egg white until stiff but not dry. Fold egg white into custard. Stir in two tablespoons of brandy. Dip lady fingers in remaining brandy and arrange on bottom of a serving dish. Combine cream cheese and coffee, beating until smooth. Spread one-third of the cream cheese mixture over the lady fingers. Spoon one-third of the custard mixture over cream cheese. Repeat layers until all ingredients are used. Refrigerate until cold. Whip cream until thick. Pipe cream on top of custard.

Serves 8 to 10.

NOTE: Custard powder is available in specialty food shops or by mail order. You can substitute an equal amount of instant vanilla pudding and pie filling mix (dry).

tiramisu and cassata (bottom)

cassata

No Italian-style cookbook would be complete without the inclusion of this popular dessert. Traditionally, cassata was made with ricotta cheese to which was added a variety of dried fruit and nuts. This mixture is used to fill a sponge cake-lined mold, then chilled. I have chosen the more "popular" interpretation of this dessert, the ice cream version.

1 quart vanilla ice cream
¼ to ½ teaspoon almond extract
1¼ cups heavy or whipping cream
2 tablespoons granulated sugar
½ cup almonds, toasted
2 ounces dark chocolate
½ cup chopped glace fruit

Soften ice cream. Stir in almond extract. Line bottom and sides of a 5-cup mold with ice cream mixture, leaving a cavity in the middle for the fruit mixture. (A metal mold is good for this recipe.) Freeze until firm. Whip cream and sugar together until peaks form. Chop almonds and chocolate. Fold glace fruit, almonds and chocolate into whipped cream. Use to fill cavity of ice cream. Cover with foil and freeze until firm. When ready to serve, dip mold into hot water very quickly two or three times, then invert and shake sharply onto a serving plate. To serve, cut into wedges.

Serves 6.

italian biscotti

Add one-half cup of shelled pistachio nuts to this recipe if you wish.

2¹/₂ ounces blanched almonds
¹/₂ cup shelled pistachios, if wished
2 cups all-purpose flour
1 teaspoon baking powder
Pinch salt
¹/₂ cup superfine granulated sugar
1 teaspoon vanilla extract
2 eggs
1 egg white

Toast almonds at 350°F for 5 to 10 minutes, or until pale golden. Allow to cool, then coarsely chop. Sift flour, baking powder and salt into a bowl. Add superfine sugar and stir until combined. Lightly beat vanilla extract and eggs together, then add to flour mixture. Mix until well combined. Turn onto a lightly floured surface and work in almonds and pistachios. Add more flour if necessary until a firm dough is reached. Divide mixture in half and shape into logs about 2 inches wide. Place on a greased baking sheet. Lightly beat egg white, then brush each log with egg white. Bake at 350°F for 35 minutes, or until cooked through. Allow to cool slightly, then cut each log on the diagonal into ¹/₂-inch-wide slices. Place slices on an ungreased baking sheet. Reduce oven temperature to 325°F and bake for 10 minutes, or until dry.

Makes about 40.

italian biscotti (left) and siena cake

siena cake

4 ounces blanched almonds
4 ounces shelled hazelnuts
$\frac{1}{2}$ cup mixed candied peel
2$\frac{1}{2}$ ounces baking chocolate
$\frac{3}{4}$ cup all-purpose flour
**2 tablespoons unsweetened cocoa
   powder**
1 teaspoon ground cinnamon
$\frac{1}{4}$ cup granulated sugar
$\frac{1}{2}$ cup honey
$\frac{1}{4}$ cup water
Confectioners' sugar

Coarsely chop almonds. Toast in a shallow baking pan at 325°F for 10 minutes, or until lightly colored. Toast hazelnuts at 325°F for 15 to 18 minutes, or until skins begin to darken. Rub to loosen skins. Remove skins and chop hazelnuts. Finely chop mixed candied peel. Coarsely chop chocolate. Sift flour, cocoa and cinnamon into a bowl. Stir in almonds, hazelnuts, chocolate and candied peel. Put sugar, honey and water in a saucepan. Stir over low heat until sugar dissolves. Increase heat and bring the mixture to the boil, stirring constantly. Boil without stirring until the soft ball stage. This is when a drop of mixture forms a soft ball in cold water. Stir sugar mixture into flour mixture until combined. Working quickly, spread batter in an 8-inch loaf pan lined with parchment or waxed paper. Smooth top with back of a wet spoon. Bake at 325°F for 35 to 40 minutes. Let cool in pan. Dust with confectioners' sugar and cut into thin wedges to serve.

Serves 10 to 12.

strawberry shortcake

You can use this idea with virtually any berries, matching the jam to suit. Try a mixture of berries for a good look.

1¹/₂ cups all-purpose flour
1 teaspoon baking powder
¹/₄ cup confectioners' sugar
³/₄ cup (1¹/₂ sticks) butter
1 egg
1 (8-ounce) carton spreadable cream cheese
¹/₄ cup confectioners' sugar
¹/₂ cup strawberry jam
2 cups fresh strawberries
¹/₂ cup granulated sugar
¹/₂ cup water

Place flour, baking powder and ¹/₄ cup confectioners' sugar in the bowl of a food processor or a bowl. Mix to combine. Cut in butter until mixture resembles fine crumbs. Add egg and a little water if necessary to make a stiff dough. Draw an 8-inch circle on parchment or waxed paper on a baking sheet. Put dough on paper and press dough out to fill the circle. Bake at 375°F for 20 to 25 minutes. Let cool. Mix cream cheese and ¹/₄ cup confectioners' sugar. Spread cream cheese mixture on cooled shortcake, then top with jam. Hull strawberries and cut in half if large. Arrange strawberries on shortcake. Heat sugar and water together over medium heat, stirring until dissolved. Increase heat and cook sugar mixture until a light golden. Remove from heat. Let cool slightly, then pour over strawberries. Working quickly, use a fork to pull threads up from caramel.

Serves 4 to 6.

strawberry shortcake

espresso

The espresso coffee machine was only invented in 1946 by Italian Achille Gaggia. Steam is forced through the coffee grounds, extracting more flavor from them than does boiling water.

Use finely ground, dark-roasted coffee for espresso flavor.

To make espresso, special equipment is required to provide the pressure to force the steam through the coffee.

Specialized electric machines are available, but there are metal pots that sit on a heating element and work very well to make a good espresso at much lower cost.

If you don't have an espresso machine of any form, use a plunger.

Espresso is served in a demi-tasse or small coffee cup.

½ cup finely ground dark-roasted coffee
½ cup boiling water

Place coffee in the bottom of a coffee plunger. Pour boiling water into plunger. Let stand for 2 minutes, then plunge. Serve immediately.

Serves 1.

mocha fino

½ cup double-strength espresso
1 tablespoon granulated sugar
1½ teaspoons unsweetened cocoa powder
1 teaspoon ground cinnamon
¼ cup milk
Additional cocoa powder, for garnish

Prepare coffee using twice the normal amount of ground coffee. Place sugar, cocoa powder and cinnamon in a large cup. Pour espresso into cup and stir. Steam milk in a Cappuccino machine or froth by blending hot milk on high speed in a blender. Pour milk into coffee. Sprinkle with additional cocoa powder.

Serves 1.

caffe latte

Caffe Latte is served in a large bowl to enable the hands to be wrapped around and warmed.

¾ cup hot strong black coffee
¾ cup hot milk

Mix coffee and milk together and pour into a coffee bowl. Serve immediately.

Serves 1.

cappuccino

If you have an espresso machine you won't need instructions on how to make a good Cappuccino. This recipe is for those who don't have a machine but enjoy good coffee.

¾ cup espresso coffee
½ cup milk
Ground cinnamon or unsweetened cocoa powder

Use an espresso blend of coffee or make the coffee by the method of your choice. Heat milk until almost boiling. Place in a blender and blend on high speed until frothy. Pour milk into coffee, spooning froth on top. Sprinkle with cinnamon or cocoa powder.

Serves 1.

from top: caffe latte, mocha fino, cappuccino and espresso

index